From VICTIM to VICTORY:

How to Recover from the Trauma and Drama of Domestic Abuse

McDougal & Associates
Servants of Christ and Stewards of the Mysteries of God

WHAT PEOPLE ARE SAYING ABOUT *FROM VICTIM TO VICTORY: HOW TO RECOVER FROM THE TRAUMA AND DRAMA OF DOMESTIC ABUSE*

"I enjoyed reading *From Victim to Victory*. It's like a set of instructions that motivates one to change his or her approach to not only domestic abuse, but to life's problems in general."

Anthony Miller
Director, Gas System of Greenville Utilities
Sunday School Superintendent of Sycamore Hill
Missionary Baptist Church
Greenville, NC

§

"*From Victim to Victory* is an easy-to-read book that provides practical advice to persons who are in abusive domestic relationships. While the author writes from the perspective of marriage, the principles shared are insightful for any person in any type of abusive relationship."

Dr. Kenneth Ray Hammond
CEO Transition Ministry Associates

§

"Through her words and her life, Jan Newell-Byrd demonstrates the power and strength that comes from waiting and listening to God when dealing with and facing toxic connections and relationships. She gives a riveting account of her personal journey from victim to victor and offers essential spiritual strategies that are necessary to achieve healing and freedom from traumatic and abusive relationships. You'll want to keep reading to see how you can gain the confidence to become a victorious overcomer."

Gloria V. Watson
Secondary English Teacher

§

"WOW! I am still basking in the glory of this wonderfully written and prayerful display of a true story, written by one of the most God-gifted and spiritually-focused women I know. I am honored to have had an early opportunity to read *From Victim to Victory*. This book is not only personally insightful, but it is filled with the Word of God that penetrates one's soul and takes you inside every experience the author writes about.

"Having grown up in a house filled with turmoil, where there was an argument or fight every day, I can relate to living in an environment where you are never at peace and can't find joy from one day to the next until you 'turn it over to God.'"

Deacon Dr. Garrie W. Moore
Retired University Administrator/Professor

§

"What a WONDERFUL book! The principles are so helpful and easy to understand. I wish this book had been available when I was in an abusive relationship. It is still a blessing in my present situation, to keep me grounded and prepared for the attacks of the enemy. I really enjoyed the book, and I can truly relate. I'm going to read it again. Praise God for you being obedient to Holy Spirit. What a blessing!"

Marlene Anderson
Director of SALT~BS Support/Care Group

§

"*From Victim to Victory: How to Recover from the Trauma and Drama of Domestic Abuse* is a must-read ,raw and personal testimony of God's sustaining power to see you through all of life's challenges. Jan Newell-Byrd offers practical and basic strategies to apply to any areas of concern in our lives and come out victorious."

Melvinna C. Wiggins, MAEd
Retired Educator
G.R. Whitfield School

"Inspiring! Empowering! Informative! This inspirational book is a 'must-read' for anyone who has had to experience struggles with domestic violence. It offers insightful strategies to overcome the emotional challenges and feelings of helplessness experienced during domestic violence encounters. The book empowers by providing insightful methods of survival and demonstrates that forgiveness is the cornerstone of rebuilding one's self-reliance, self-sufficiency, and self-esteem. As stated by Bernard Williams, 'Man has never made any material as resilient as the human spirit.' This book is a testimony to that spirit."

Gloria F. Snead ,Ed.D

§

"This book is a 'must read' for any person who desires to experience complete, holistic healing from domestic abuse. At a time when domestic violence is spiraling out of control, it offers simple, yet comprehensive advice for victims of this malady, which is so pervasive and entrenched in our society. Jan's honesty and willingness to share her personal experiences on this subject gives the book an authentic appeal, not just to victims, but to anyone desiring to increase their awareness. It is easy to read and understand, regardless of your level of education. It addresses the issue of domestic abuse at its core, lays bare its damaging effects upon one's humanity, and offers advice that can aid in putting victims on a permanent path to recovery by tapping into the greatest power source available—God."

Erma McCray McAdory
Facilitator, Codependent Support Group

§

"*From Victim to Victory* leverages the personal account of Reverend Newell-Byrd's 64-year entanglement with domestic abuse to rise above [in spite of it]. With each word, she beckons a sense of calmness. The words are a source of inspiration, encouragement, and strength to men and women who continue to navigate their journey to restoration."

Ursula Belle, President
Greenville (NC) Alumnae Chapter
Delta Sigma Theta Sorority, Inc
2019-2021

§

"Jan's honesty and vulnerability goes to her heart that wants to help others trapped in domestic violence. Her desire is to help people get physically, emotionally, and spiritually free. In this book, she reveals the clear and concise strategies that the Lord gave her so that she can live in freedom today. This freedom then allows her to be a vessel the Lord Jesus uses to help others to become free themselves. I love Jan's overcoming story and her heart to help others overcome!"

Reverend Jay Buckingham
Covenant Church

§

"*From Victim to Victory* is a perfect addition to rehabilitation programs for survivors of domestic violence. The Rev. Dr. Jan Newell-Byrd has lived it, not just studied it, and is uniquely qualified to present this interesting combination of scripture, practical experience, and Bible study.

"Every counselor of female survivors of domestic violence will want a copy of *From Victim to Victory* in their rehabilitation arsenal. Every woman seeking to emerge victorious from the horrors of domestic abuse will rejoice for the gift the Lord has anointed Rev. Jan to provide. It's a must-read for those striving to break the chains of bondage."

Adriawa Evans
Lifelong Learner and Repeat Sinner

§

"*From Victim to Victory* is a wonderful book for those who find themselves in an abusive relationship. The strategies are tremendous tips that will assist in becoming victors in any given situation—physical, mental, or even self-abuse. Jan's testimony and her life is a terrific example of how you don't have to remain in the state you are in. God can and will make a way!"

Elizabeth Blount
2016-2020, First-Vice President
Greenville (NC) Alumnae Chapter
Delta Sigma Theta Sorority, Inc.

§

"Self-knowledge is an obtainable blessing. Jan Newell Byrd's, *FROM VICTIM TO VICTORY* is an inspiring and wonderful writing that defines how overcoming is within reach through divine direction."

Dennis Branch
Retired Consultant

§

We have the keys! Rev. Jan's timely and Spirit-inspired work provides a step-by-step process for moving from trauma and abuse to a victorious life. Her testimony of rising from *FROM VICTIM TO VICTORY* empowers those impacted by domestic violence, as well as any reader, to become their most liberated selves through faith and determination. Page by page, she masterfully teaches how to approach the throne of grace and how to use prayer as a weapon of war to tear down strongholds, and shares unforgettable wisdom milestones and teachings as a woman of faith ordained by our Lord and Savior Jesus Christ. This is a must-read for all who dare to be their best selves."

The Reverend Carolyn J. Fleming-Dockery
J.D., ACPE Educator

§

"*From Victim to Victory* is a must read to fully understand how the author has been victorious. It is what I term her 'scriptural survival guide.'"

Mildred Moore Daniels
Social Work Supervisor III (Retired)
Greenville (NC) Alumnae
Delta Sigma Theta Sorority, Inc.

§

"This book clearly lays out biblical principles that will guide you to success, as you journey through the process *From Victim to Victory*."

Sherry Johnson
Administrative Assistant

"What an honor to review your new book! You have such a gift of capturing, not only your story, but giving practical examples of how to listen and obey the voice of God. The actual strategies provided are perfect, not only for someone who is or has been a victim of domestic violence, but for everyone who desires to live a Spirit-led life."

Tonya Edwards,
Communications Director, Covenant Church

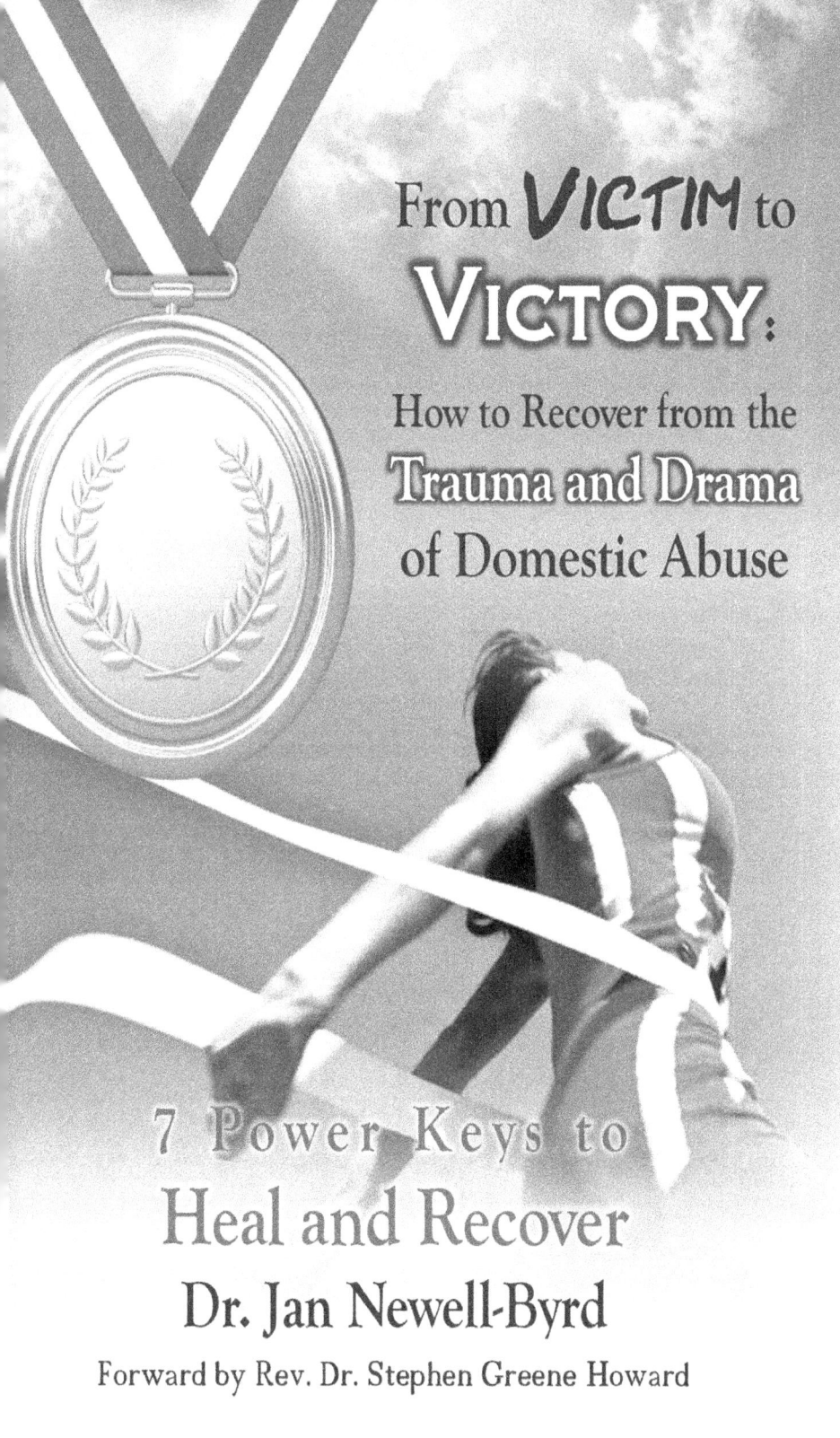

From Victim to Victory
Copyright © 2020, 2021 by Jan Newell-Byrd.
ALL RIGHTS RESERVED.

Unless otherwise noted, all Scripture references are from *The Holy Bible, New International Version*, copyright © 1973, 1978, 1984, 2011 by Biblica, Colorado Springs, Colorado. References marked NKJV are from *The Holy Bible, New King James Version*, copyright © 1979, 1980, 1982, 1990 by Thomas Nelson, Inc., Nashville, Tennessee. References marked MSG are from *The Message*, copyright © 1993, 1994, 1995, 1996, 2000, 2002 by NavPress Publishing Group, Colorado Springs, Colorado. References marked NLT are from *The Holy Bible, New Living Translation*, copyright © 1996, 2004, 2007 by Tyndale House Foundation. Used by permission of Tyndale House Publishers, Inc., Carol Stream, Illinois. References marked ESV are from the *The Holy Bible, English Standard Version*, copyright © 2001 by Crossway Bibles, a publishing ministry of Good News Publishers. References marked KJV are from *The Holy Bible, King James Version*, public domain. References marked AMP are from *The Amplified Bible*, copyright © 2015 by The Lockman Foundation, La Habra, California. References marked "TLB" are from *The Living Bible* paraphrased by Kenneth Taylor, copyright © 1971 by Tyndale House Publishers, Inc., Wheaton, Illinois. References marked NASB are from the *New American Standard Bible*, copyright © 1960, 1962, 1963, 1968, 1971, 1972, 1973, 1975, 1977 by the Lockman Foundation, La Habra, California. References marked NRS are from the *New Revised Standard Version of the Bible*, copyright © 1989, by the Division of Christian Education of the National Council of Churches of Christ in the United States of America. References marked GW are from *GOD'S WORD Translation*, copyright © 1995 by God's Word to the Nations. Used by permission of God's Word Mission Society. References marked RSV are from *The Revised Standard Version of the Bible*, copyright © 1946, 1952, 1971, 1973 by the Division of Christian Education of the National Council of the Churches of Christ in the U.S.A. References marked ISV are from *The International Standard Version of the Bible*, copyright © 1995-2014 by ISV Foundation. ALL RIGHTS RESERVED INTERNATIONALLY. Used by permission of Davidson Press, LLC. References marked MEV are from *The Holy Bible, Modern English Version*, copyright © 2014 by Military Bible Association. Published and distributed by Charisma House. References marked ICB are from *The Holy Bible, International Children's Bible*® Copyright© 1986, 1988, 1999, 2015 by Tommy Nelson™, a division of Thomas Nelson. Used by permission. References marked WEB are from the World English Bible™, public domain.

Cover design by Mia Eley

Published by:

McDougal & Associates
18896 Greenwell Springs Road
Greenwell Springs, LA 70739

www.ThePublishedWord.com

McDougal & Associates is an organization dedicated to the spreading of the Gospel of the Lord Jesus Christ to as many people as possible in the shortest time possible.

ISBN: 978-1-950398-21-8

Printed on demand in the U.S., the U.K. and Australia
For Worldwide Distribution

Dedication

To my Lord and Savior Jesus Christ, who protected my life during the many years I lived in fear as a victim of domestic abuse.

To all the men and women who have ever had their dignity challenged by an abuser.

To the many advocates who continue to seek solutions to the pervasive problems of domestic abuse.

Acknowledgements

To my adult children, S. Wesley Newell, Mark Anthony Newell, and Ronda Janis Byrd, who lived through my trauma and drama, for their unconditional love and encouragement.

To my grandchildren, Morgan, Melani, Jeremiah, and Ashlynn, for their sweet love and devotion.

To my daughter-in-law, Dana, for her strength of character and encouragement.

To my sister, Ada, for sharing her wisdom and insight.

To my readers and perusers: Gertha Crumpler, Soror Karen Harding, Lola Thompson, Teff Sheets, and Paulette Smallwood.

To Della Dixon, special gratitude and appreciation for her tenacity, attention to detail, and for volunteering to read the entire manuscript.

Above all others, to the Holy Spirit through Jesus Christ, who birthed and authored both books and enabled me to serve as His secretary. I humbly and gratefully submit to His will.

Disclaimer

From Victim to Victory: How to Recover from the Trauma and Drama of Domestic Abuse is a how-to book, a blueprint, a guide. The experiences of the author qualify her as an expert and primary source after successfully enduring and overcoming the victimization of domestic violence and emotional and verbal abuse for more than forty-two years (almost two decades with Husband Number One and twenty-two years with Husband Number Two) without her becoming bitter and angry. She recovered victoriously. Nevertheless, the contents of this book are not designed or intended to take the place of a marriage and family counseling service. This is one woman's journey.

The principles and strategies described in this book were given to the author by God and worked successfully for her, but they may or may not function the same way for the reader. However, God is faithful. He will give you your own unique principles and solutions if you ask Him (see James 1:5).

Contents

Foreword by Rev. Dr. Stephen Greene Howard 18

Introduction 21

Power Key # 1—Be PRAYERFUL 25
   Strategies 36
Power Key # 2—Be WISE 42
   Strategies 52
Power Key # 3—Be VERBAL (Say Something) 57
   Strategies 76
Power Key # 4—Be FORGETFUL (Intentionally) 81
   Strategies 93
Power Key # 5—Be VIGILANT (not Gaslighted) 100
   Strategies 112
Power Key # 6—Be FORGIVING 124
   Strategies 139
Power Key # 7—Be VICTORIOUS 145
   Strategies 158

Questions for Reflection and Group Discussion 170

EPILOGUE **173**
   The Spiritual Conversion and Transformation of Husband Number One, a Former Domestic Violence Abuser

SPECIAL FEATURES **185**
   What Is Real Love? 187
   Why Does She Stay? 191
   Battered Men 201
   Seven Priceless Principles 214
   Six Steps on the Romans Road to Salvation 219

   Author Contact Page 225

Foreword by Rev. Dr. Stephen Greene Howard

There are many books written about domestic violence, but there are not many that combine real originality and selflessness with intellectual integrity like the author of this book. The Rev. Dr. Jan Newell-Byrd, in her second printed and published literary work, has combined her personal life experiences, her faith walk with God, and her triumph through God's matchless grace. While her previous work, *Testimony of a Kept Woman: From Misery to Ministry Instead of the Penitentiary*, is a classic, *From Victim to Victory* not only demonstrates indebtedness to the classic, but is an empowering tool for others for recovery from drama and abuse.

The statistics of abuse in the Body of Christ are alarming as they have hit both national and global heights. Aaron Earls, as quoted by, *Life*, gives five myths of domestic violence in the Body of Christ. These myths are as follows: 1). It doesn't happen in Christian homes. 2). Submission will solve the problem. 3). It's the woman's fault. 4). Domestic abuse is not as bad as domestic violence, and 5). If the abuser is truly sorry and forgiven, the relationship should be reconciled. Dr. Newell, in

Foreword by Rev. Dr. Stephen Greene Howard

this book, not only dispels the myths, but also offers the path of recovery, discovering who and whose you are.

It has been my delight and joy to do ministry alongside this great champion of the faith, whose desire and passion is to share her painful ordeal to empower others. Her work and testimony speak volumes of her deep-rooted faith that sustained and delivered her from forty-two years of abuse.

Rev. Dr. Jan Newell-Byrd has tapped into a significant hidden area of Christendom and is challenging the church today to see, feel, and hear the cries, tears, and pain of those in the fold. Her work takes roots in the heart of the church and must be attended to.

A few months ago, I was blessed by the words of scripture as found in the book of Genesis, revealing how a devout patriarch of the faith practiced violence and abuse in his own home, and I was encouraged to speak for those who can't speak for themselves. This is a cause I am honored to bear and grateful that God has raised God's servant, Jan, to lead the way. She leads as a wounded healer and declares, "I'm not a victim but a victor."

The greatest problems of our time are not technology, politics, nor economics. The greatest problems are moral and spiritual. Unless we make progress in these areas, we are all doomed. Reading this powerful and insightful literary work will aid us all in avoiding the doom and creating a wholesome, functioning society.

Thanks, Dr. Newell-Byrd, for such a wonderful gift. Out of the ashes of violence, God, through you and countless unknowns, is building a new nation.

Dr. Stephen Greene Howard, Senior Pastor
Cornerstone Missionary Baptist Church
Greenville, NC

INTRODUCTION

For many years, I was a victim of domestic abuse. I wrote a book entitled *Testimony of a Kept Woman: From Misery to Ministry Instead of the State Penitentiary.* In my memoir, I shared my experiences of what went on behind closed doors as a victim of both physical violence and emotional and verbal abuse.

I want to thank those who read my first book and shared their comments with me. Several of you said you were blessed and encouraged by my openness, honesty, and willingness to share my life experiences. Others expressed the need to know more about how I recovered because they were still struggling and unable to move on to complete healing and restoration. The essential questions most readers asked were: How was it possible for me to recover from forty-two years of domestic violence and emotional and verbal abuse? How did I transcend the pain and agony of abuse and not become angry or bitter? More importantly, how was I able to move from victim to victory and become transformed into a successful survivor and overcomer? The answers to those questions and how my life was changed are found in this sequel: *From Victim to Victory: How to Recover from the Trauma and Drama of Domestic Abuse.*

This is a how-to book or guide that does not necessarily have to be read in sequential order. It gives the principles and strategies that enabled me to recover and become a victorious overcomer after forty-two years (almost two decades with Husband Number One and twenty-two years with Husband Number Two) of being a victim of domestic abuse. These principles and strategies helped me to successfully recover and overcome domestic violence and emotional and verbal abuse without becoming angry and bitter. This is the journey of a restored woman.

The problems of domestic abuse are similar, but no two situations are exactly alike. The strategies that God used with me may or may not necessarily be the same strategies He will use with you. God is sovereign. Therefore, do not be surprised or disappointed if God does things differently with you than He did with me. God created you and knows what is best for you (see Psalm 100:3). He will give you solutions specifically designed for your unique problems, if you ask Him (see James 1:5).

Introduction

Included in this new book are excerpts from my first book, *Testimony of a Kept Woman: From Misery to Ministry Instead of the State Penitentiary*. Please refer to the pages indicated for greater clarity and understanding of my journey through the trials of domestic abuse. The names of characters have been changed to protect the identity of my two ex-husbands and others.

Five Special Features are included in this book:

- What is Real Love?
- Why Does She Stay?
- Battered Men: The Silent Victims in Domestic Abuse
- Seven Priceless Principles: How to Raise Functional Children in a Dysfunctional Environment
- Six Steps on the Roman Road to Salvation

My goals for writing this book have been threefold:

1. To provide awareness to the pervasive nature of domestic abuse
2. To encourage and empower victims of domestic abuse (both males and females)
3. To recommend principles and strategies to those seeking solutions to their problems

From Victim to Victory

From Victim to Victory: How to Recover from the Trauma and Drama of Domestic Abuse is a book for anyone who has ever had his or her dignity and self-worth challenged by an abuser. May the Lord Jesus Christ be glorified and all former victims of abuse edified, as we move triumphantly together *From Victim to Victory*! Read, reflect, and recover!

To God be the glory!
Jan Newell-Byrd

Ye shall know the truth, and the truth shall make you free. John 8:32, KJV

No matter who you are or what you have done, God loves you with a perfect *agape* love (see 1 John 4:8).

As the Lord was with Joseph
(Genesis Chapters 37-50),
so has the Lord been with Jan!

POWER KEY #1

BE PRAYERFUL

I tell you, you can pray for anything, and if you believe that you've received it, it will be yours.
Jesus in Mark 11:24, NLT

To move from victim to victory and recover from the trauma and drama of domestic abuse, one must first be prayerful.

WHAT IS PRAYER?

Prayer is talking to God, then listening and waiting for God to speak back to you. Prayer is a two-way conversation, not a one-way monologue. The most difficult part of prayer is learning to wait, listen, and discern the voice of God.

I believe in prayer. Even before I clearly understood what real prayer was, I talked with God almost every day. There were times when I even got down on my knees and poured out my heart's desire and most profound concerns to God. In a smug kind of way, I was pretty proud of myself for taking the time to pray. After all, I realized that most people don't pray at all (even church folks). Yes, I "talked" to God, but that was all I did. It was years before I learned to wait and listen for Him to talk back to me.

God's voice is not a natural voice that I hear with my natural ear. It's more like a sixth sense or thoughts coming into my mind. God's voice is hard to explain and define, but what a difference it made for me when I realized that the All-Wise and Omnipotent God of the Universe would actually want to commune and speak with me. It was a life-changing revelation!

What Is Marriage?

Marriage is a covenant ordained by God. Marriage was His idea. He is the Creator and Originator of holy matrimony. Marriage is a sacred bond between one man and one woman united by God in the most intimate of all human relationships (see Genesis 2:24-25).

I believe in marriage. It was always my desire to marry once and live happily ever after ... until death do us part. However, my life turned out very differently. Never in my wildest imagination would I have predicted that I would marry, not once, but twice, and also divorce twice, ending up a victim of domestic abuse—both physical violence and emotional and verbal abuse. But that is precisely what happened to me.

KNOWLEDGE IS POWER

Ignorance is not bliss, and what you don't know *can* hurt you. I have been severely hurt by what I didn't know. As important as prayer is, I'm amazed at how little I prayed. For example, I don't remember praying about my decision to marry Vincent, Husband Number One. Marriage is the most important commitment one can ever make in life, and yet, I am not sure if I prayed about that decision. Isn't that's incredible?

Worse than that, even if I did pray, I know I never waited long enough to hear God's response to my prayer. Frankly, at the age of nineteen, I didn't know enough about prayer to even expect God to respond to my request. Unfortunately, I paid a high price for my ignorance. Perhaps much of the drama and trauma of domestic abuse in my life could have been avoided if I had not only learned how to talk and ask God questions, but also how to wait and listen for His answers in prayer.

Yes, it's true. Ignorance is not bliss, and what you don't know can hurt you. Knowledge is power.

What Is Domestic Abuse or Domestic Violence?

Domestic violence is a pattern of negative and adverse behavior used by one partner to maintain power and control over the other partner through fear, mind control, intimidation, and manipulation. It includes physical violence, psychological violence, and emotional and verbal abuse.

Domestic violence doesn't look the same in every relationship because every relationship is different. One thing most abusive relationships have in common is that the abusive partner will do whatever is necessary to maintain power and control over his or her victim.

Does the Bible Address the Problem of Domestic Abuse?

Yes, God has lots to say about marriage and domestic abuse in His Word. Sadly, for many years, I didn't know this. All that time, I was miserable, unhappy, and depressed as a victim. I would pray, cry out to the Lord, and say, "God, where are You as I am being abused in domestic violence?" "God, why don't You answer my prayer when I cry out to You?" "Lord God, do You really care?" Even though I didn't know it at the time, the answers to my questions were, "Yes, God really does care, and He does hear our cries to Him."

As I sought for answers in my desperation, I learned that God is personally interested in every problem I have, especially a problem of domestic abuse. I learned that the Lord not only cares about me, a victim of domestic abuse, but He loves me, and He wants to protect and preserve my life. He will make a way of escape.

Does God Always Answer Prayers Immediately?

No, the Lord God does not always answer our prayers immediately. His divine schedule is not on our schedule. I know that because I prayed one particular prayer year after year, and nothing happened. I asked the Lord to change my husband and make him a better man. Instead of changing Vincent, the Lord changed me. Amazingly, thirty-one years later, God answered my long-delayed prayer in the most unbelievable and incredible way. David prayed:

> *Hear me when I call, O God of my righteousness: you have enlarged me when I was in distress; have mercy on me and hear my prayer.* Psalm 4:1, KJV

From the very beginning, Vincent and I were total opposites. Yes, it's true that opposites attract, but they later repel. We had very few things in common. For example, I loved people, but Vincent didn't. I had a close relationship with my family, especially my mother and Vincent's. I called his mother "Mom," and she called me her daughter-in-love. On the other hand, Vincent and his mother had a strained and distant relationship. They didn't get along at all.

Vincent's dislike for people and his anti-social behavior made him miserable at work and at home, and the result was that he went into dark moods of hostility and anger and became increasingly more violent. As our sons, Dexter and Lawrence, grew older, they began to jump between us to intervene in our altercations to protect me.

I may be slow, but I wasn't completely dense. I could see the proverbial handwriting on the wall. Then came the last straw. Finally, I was shaken to the core of my being, and I found the courage, strength, and sense to get up and leave.

Continuing a Close Relationship with My Ex-In-Laws

I divorced Vincent, but I did not divorce his family. Although we separated in 1976 and later divorced, strange as it seems, Vincent's mother and I continued to have a close relationship. She knew about her son's problems, but we never once discussed them. It's weird, but in those days, many people buried their heads in the sand and pretended their problems did not exist (even when they did). I knew it saddened my mother-in-law that I was no longer married to her son, but that's how it had to be. Enough was enough!

Be Prayerful

In 2007, at the age of ninety-eight, when Vincent's mother knew she was about to die, she called me and asked that I attend her funeral with her two grandsons. She had continued to live in Philadelphia and, at the time, we lived in other states. When she finally passed away, Dexter, Lawrence and I flew to Philadelphia to attend her funeral. Vincent refused to attend his own mother's funeral. I was totally disgusted with him for this and vowed to never speak to him again. But the Holy Spirit had different plans.

DEFIANT, THEN OBEDIENT

Soon after I returned home from the funeral, the Holy Spirit began to gently but persistently speak to me in that quiet and still voice. The Spirit of God told me to call Vincent and witness to him over the phone. I was shocked and confused that the Lord would demand that I reach out to a man who had been so mean and insensitive to his own mother. At first, I tried to ignore this Voice. I was totally resistant to the idea that God would ask me to do something that I was so opposed to doing.

Secondly, God knew that I hadn't seen or heard from Vincent since I had left him in Gary, Indiana in 1976. What if Vincent wouldn't even answer the phone or talk to me? After five or six weeks, I was eventually obedient to God's voice and made the call.[1]

---
1. See *Testimony of a Kept Woman*, pp.237-243

From Victim to Victory

God's Amazing Grace

It's amazing, but God did the unbelievable! After witnessing to Vincent over the phone for more than two hours, he prayed the prayer of salvation, accepted the Lord Jesus Christ as His Savior, and became born again. Instantly, he was transformed and became a brand-new man. He began to cry! And then he laughed out loud! And then he apologized over and over again to me for how he had mistreated me all those years. It was truly a miracle! Vincent's transformation was as dramatic and miraculous as the conversion of Saul of Tarsus on the Road to Damascus in Acts 9. I was shocked and overjoyed!

In Prayer, God's Delay Is Not God's Denial

For years I had prayed to God to change Vincent, but the Lord didn't seem to answer my prayer. Nothing ever seemed to change that man. But, the Lord *did* answer my prayer—thirty-one years after Vincent and I had divorced. Incredible! It is true that God does not always answer when we want Him to, but the Lord will *always* answer.

God is Always Faithful

The next day I sent Vincent a Bible, and for the next ten years, we studied the Bible together over the phone on the last Sunday of every month at 4:00 PM. It was absolutely incredible! Only the Lord Jesus Christ could have changed Vincent from a physically violent domestic abuser into a Bible-loving, gentle man who made peace with me and his two sons and bonded with his two granddaughters. God is amazing!

WHAT A COMICAL QUESTION: WOULD I MARRY HIM AGAIN?

An old friend of mine heard the good news about the miraculous transformation of Vincent, Husband Number One. She was excited and couldn't believe her ears. She had known the "old" Vincent years earlier, when we were all in college together. Even back then, he had a reputation that was not very flattering. When my friend and I recently met up together, she asked me a question that was in her heart and mind. She said, "Jan, now that Vincent is a changed man, and he is no longer physically violent or abusive, do you think you might marry him again?" It's a good thing I wasn't eating because I nearly choked when she said that!

I laughed and said, "Absolutely not! Yes, I'm thankful the Lord saved my former husband, but to marry Vincent again would be totally out of the question. No way! Besides, all of our interactions had been done over the phone. I hadn't seen Vincent since 1976. I didn't even know what he looked like. The answer is no!"

We both had a good laugh and then changed the subject.

To God be the Glory!

— An Important Question —

How will you recover from the trauma and drama of emotional domestic violence and move from victim to victory?

Strategies

Strategy #1: Be Prayerful

Prayer is essential to becoming whole again.

> *They should always pray and never give up.*
> *Luke 18:1, NLT*

The Lord will equip you with the capacity to pray your way through.

> *Then you will call on me and come and pray to me, and I will listen to you.*
> *Jeremiah 29:12*

> *Call to me, and I will answer you and tell you great and unsearchable things you do not know.*
> *Jeremiah 33:3*

What a blessing to be a blessing! And it all happened because I learned to be prayerful.

Strategy #2: Prayer is Optional, But Consequences Are Not

Strategies

Prayer is a choice. You don't have to pray, and God won't stand over you and make you pray. The Lord has given each of us free will to decide to do what we feel is best. But we are not allowed to determine the consequences of our choices.

Strategy #3: Pray or Worry, But You Can't Do Both

Do not worry about anything, but in every situation, by prayer and petition, with thanksgiving, present your requests to God. And the peace of God, which transcends all understanding, will guard your hearts and your minds in Christ Jesus. Philippians 4:6-7

Strategy #4: Sing or Hum the Words of Old Hymns for Encouragement

Whenever you are depressed or stressed, try humming or singing your favorite hymn. It's like putting a prayer to music. For example:

What a Friend We Have in Jesus

What a Friend we have in Jesus?
All our sins and griefs to bear,
What a privilege to carry

everything to God in prayer.
O what peace we often forfeit,
O what needless pain we bear,
All because we do not carry,
everything to God in prayer.[2]

For God so loved the world that He gave His only begotten Son, that whoever believes in Him should not perish, but have everlasting life. John 3:16, **NKJV**

Strategy #5: Understand that You Have Power in Christ Jesus (see Psalm 139:14-18)

One of the most significant problems with domestic abuse is that it is more of a spiritual problem than a personal problem, and unless the solution is approached spiritually, complete recovery and healing will never come.

Begin to place a high premium on yourself as the temple of the Living God and take care of yourself:

Put on the whole armor of God, that you may be able to stand against the wiles of the devil. For we do not wrestle against flesh and blood, but against principali-

---

2. Written by Charles Crozat Converse and Joseph Scrivenm lyrics © Warner Chappell Music, Inc, Universal Music Publishing Group, Downtown Music Publishing, Kobalt Music Publishing Ltd., BMG Rights Management, O/B/O Capasso, Bluewater Music Corp., Songtrust Ave

ties, against powers, against the rulers of the darkness of this age, against spiritual hosts of wickedness in the heavenly places. Ephesians 6:11-12 , NKJV

Strategy #6: Know that "With God, All Things Are Possible" (Matthew 19:26)

You may be struggling with the challenges of domestic violence and emotional and verbal abuse, and it may seem that you don't have the answers and that your situation will never improve. Just keep praying and listening to the still small voice of the Holy Spirit. He is wisdom and truth. He has the solutions to your problems. Maintain the faith. Stay in the Word and on your knees, and do whatever He tells you to do.

Now to Him who is able to do exceedingly abundantly above all that we ask or think, according to the power that works in us. Ephesians 3:20, NKJV

The Victor's Prayer

Dear Heavenly Father,
Teach me to pray.
I need You to help me.
Bless me, Lord Jesus.
Enable me to be all that You
have ordained me to be.
I will give You praise and glory.
Thank You, Lord.

In Jesus name, I pray.
Amen!

Be Prayerful

> *Ye shall know the truth, and the truth shall make you free.* John 8:32, KJV

No matter who you are, or what you have done, God loves you with a perfect (*agape*) love (see 1 John 4:8).

As the Lord was with Joseph
(Genesis Chapters 37-50),
so has the Lord been with Jan!

Power Key #2

BE WISE

If any of you lacks wisdom, you should ask God, who gives generously to all without finding fault, and it will be given to you.   James 1:5

To move from victim to victory and recover from the trauma and drama of domestic abuse, one must be wise.

WHAT IS WISDOM? AND WHERE DOES WISDOM COME FROM?

According to the dictionary, *wisdom* is "the ability to think and act using knowledge, experience, understanding, common sense, and insight." Wisdom comes from the Lord. It begins and ends with the fear of God. Where there is no fear of the Lord, there can never be any real wisdom. This fear isn't the kind of fear one has of being struck by lightning or of being killed some other way. No, wisdom is a deep, abiding, holy respect for the Lord and for His Word, the Bible.

Be Wise

Wisdom is not automatic. There are many smart and intelligent people in the world. Some people are brilliant and have high IQs, but they may or may not be wise. Their lives may be catastrophic because they don't know how to get along with other people, and they have no peace. On the other hand, some individuals aren't what we would call "intellectuals." They may or may not have a degree of higher education, and yet they possess wisdom or a sixth sense that enables them to instinctively know what to do and what not to do. The result is that they live a peaceful and orderly life. We would say that one has wisdom and the other does not.

Wisdom and information are different. Information and facts are taught in school, using books and other sources, but wisdom and understanding come from the Lord and His Word. Unfortunately, the Bible is no longer taught in our public schools, and most people do not have wisdom. Smarts? Yes! Wisdom? No!

I was a victim of both domestic violence and emotional and verbal abuse, and I lacked wisdom. Many of the problems I experienced in my two marriages were because I did not pray and ask the Lord to lead and guide me. I was operating on my own understanding, which was less than zero (see Proverbs 3:7).

After failing and repeating the same mistakes over and over again, I became frustrated and anxious, and in my desperation,

From Victim to Victory

I turned to God's Word. I had heard that the book of Proverbs was written by Solomon, the son of King David and the wisest man who ever lived. That book of Proverbs has more to say about wisdom than any other book in the Bible.

Proverbs was written like a calendar. There are thirty-one chapters, one for each day of the month. So, I made a decision to read one chapter each day on the corresponding day of the month. For example, if it was the third day of the month, I read Proverbs 3. If it was the tenth day of the month, I read Proverbs 10. Each day I tried to read a chapter. Now and then, I would miss reading a chapter, but that was not a problem. The Holy Spirit would not allow me to "beat myself up" over it (see Romans 8:1). The next time I remembered to read, I simply read the chapter that was the same day of the month.

Before long, I was reading a chapter of Proverbs each day or night. Slowly, but surely, I began to notice a change in how I felt and how I was starting to think. It was a real improvement. I also found that if I prayed before I read the Scriptures, I tended to remember more of the verses I read, and it was easier for me to apply some of what I remembered to my everyday situations.

Then, as I was forming a habit of reading the Scriptures, I began using colored highlighters to underline scriptures that resonated with me. I even began to write notes on what

I was learning. By the end of two or three months, I found the book of Proverbs to be easy to read and understand. By the end of the sixth month of reading Proverbs, I found that I was able to memorize some short verses, and God's words were coming back to my remembrance when I needed them the most throughout the day. God is so awesome!

TOXIC PEOPLE WILL DRIVE YOU CRAZY!
I needed God's wisdom to help me deal with the two toxic men I married. I found out the hard way that living with toxic people will drive you crazy. To make matters worse, I had started to fake my own sense of reality to endure what I was going through. Yes, I agree with you. That is insane! But, like many, it was not easy for me to understand and know how to relate to the erratic and unreasonable behavior of these toxic men. The more I tried to change myself to be what they wanted me to be (and, thus, please them) the worse my life became.

My problem was that I was always trying to fix my toxic husbands, when what I needed to do was fix my own unrealistic outlook on life. What I did not realize is that toxic people don't want to be helped. They want to change you and use you for their needs. They have twisted purposes and totally irrational behavior. I desperately needed God's wisdom, and the Lord was beginning to give it to me.

TRANSFORMED BY WISDOM.

I was gaining wisdom from reading Proverbs. I also read the book of Romans. Reading Romans 12:2 changed me:

> *Don't copy the behavior and customs of this world, but let God transform you into a new person by changing the way you think. Then you will learn to know God's will for you, which is good and pleasing and perfect.* (TLB)

I had made many mistakes in my life, but God was beginning to give me His wisdom. God's love was empowering me to take responsibility for my life. It was as if I had been sleep walking all those years. I now walked in His power, and I would worship Him with my whole heart.

I also read Ephesians 6:10-18 over and over. God was giving wisdom and discernment to know what to do in all the situations in my life experience of domestic violence. The Holy Spirit was teaching me how to prepare and dress for danger.

DEALING WITH A SWITCHBLADE KNIFE

It was no secret that Vincent had a terrible temper, and he could lash out at me in a split second over nothing. And, of course, I was aware that he had that dangerous 18-inch, pearl-handled switchblade knife he had brought back home from Germany. He kept it in a drawer in our bedroom. What made matters worse, Vincent was proud of his knife, and occasionally he would go to the bureau drawer where he kept it, take it out, look at it, admire it, and then return it to the drawer. I had often wondered what would happen if he got so angry he would use that weapon he kept in the bureau drawer.

Not only did I hate knives, but I was deathly afraid of them. For some unknown reason, knives terrified me much more than guns. Logically, I reasoned that a person could shoot you from a distance. But to be stabbed, the assailant would have to get close enough to his victim to carry out the malicious deed. Knives made my flesh crawl. One night I dreamed that something horrible was about to happen with Vincent's knife. I took that dream as a warning from God. The Lord was giving me wisdom.

Obedience Saved My Life

The next morning, I was still shaken by my dream. As I stood looking out the kitchen window of our second-floor apartment, I began to ponder verses from the book of Proverbs I had memorized, my favorite scripture:

> *Trust in the LORD with all thine heart; and lean not unto thine own understanding. In all thy ways acknowledge him, and he shall direct thy path.*
>
> Proverbs 3:5-6, KJV

As I recited that scripture, the Lord spoke to me, almost in an audible voice. He told me to get rid of the knife. As I continued to stand staring out the window, I heard the city trash truck noisily rolling down the street.

Back in those days, the trash was collected in an open dump truck. Two men would pick up the individual trash containers on the street curb, hoist them up high, and throw the trash in them into the open truck bed as the third man drove the truck. Immediately, I knew what I had to do. I turned, went into our bedroom, opened Vincent's bureau drawer, found the switchblade knife, took it out, and went back to the kitchen and opened the door.

By this time, the trash truck had reached our apartment building, and I could clearly see where to throw the knife. The men who were collecting the trash had their backs turned, as they went to empty the full trash cans on the curb. I said a prayer, took aim, and threw the knife. It landed perfectly in the pile of trash on the back of the truck and quickly sank down to the bottom.

I stood rooted to that spot on the second-floor landing, as the trash truck slowly moved up the street and, eventually, out of sight. I sighed a big sigh of relief. I had acted in obedience to the Lord's warning and felt an unusual sense of peace and safety. I felt uplifted and free. I was exercising God's wisdom.

Be Wise

BETTER CAREFUL THAN SORRY

Several days later, the boys or I did something (what exactly it was, I can't remember), but Vincent became agitated and irritated with us. He began to yell profanities and paced up and down the floor. Suddenly, he turned, went into the bedroom, opened his bureau drawer, and reached for his pearl-handled, 18-inch switchblade knife. This time, the knife wasn't there. He couldn't find it. He swore and felt around for it again, but he didn't feel anything. In desperation, he snatched the drawer out of the bureau and emptied the entire contents of it on the floor in search of the knife, but it was nowhere to be found. All the while he was cursing and calling everything a "blankety-blank-blank!"

The toxic man was furious, but he was also confused. The knife had always been there, but he had never reached to take it out before in anger. That day, in a violent fit of rage, he had reached for it with the intention of hurting me, and the knife was gone! Thank God, His wisdom had pre-warned me, and I had gotten rid of that weapon.

Vincent looked at me with a dazed and puzzled look on his face, as if to say, "I know that dummy wouldn't have the sense or the nerve to get rid of my knife." He just stared at me. Amazingly, he calmed down just as quickly as he had become agitated, pulled himself together, sat down, and watched television.

God literally saved my life because I had learned to trust in the Lord and listen to His still, small voice.

Thank You for Your divine wisdom, my Lord and Savior Jesus Christ.

TO GOD BE THE GLORY!

— **AN IMPORTANT QUESTION** —

How did I recover from the trauma and drama of physical domestic violence and move from victim to victory?

Strategies

Strategy # 1: Choose To Be Wise

Read your Bible, especially the book of Proverbs. Read and teach Proverbs to your children. It will give them the wisdom and understanding they need to prepare them for a good life.

Strategy # 2: Decide Not to Stay Longer than Necessary

Realize that it is not the Lord's will for you to live in constant chaos and fear.

> *For the Spirit God gave us does not make us timid, but it gives us power, love, and self-discipline.*
>
>   2 Timothy 1:7

Allow yourself to be transformed into a courageous woman of faith. Feel God's presence. Be empowered to overcome your low self-esteem.

Do not remain in a violent situation any longer than necessary, and do not allow guilt and condemnation to keep you in mental chains. There is no condemnation in Christ Jesus (see Romans 8:1).

Confess your sin and move on. Jesus has already paid the price for you. Don't continue "beating yourself up" for what you did years ago. Hear God's voice and LET GO OF THE PAST!

Strategy # 3: Identify Toxic People

With God's wisdom, detect and identify the erratic and unreasonable behavior of toxic people. Learn to spot them and avoid them at all costs. For the sake of your emotional safety and mental sanity, turn and run for the hills.

Strategy # 4: Develop a Keen Sense of Spiritual Wisdom and Awareness.

Fools rush in where wise men fear to tread. Take your time and learn from your past mistakes.

> *If any of you lacks wisdom, you should ask God, who gives generously to all without finding fault, and it will be given to you.*   James 1:5

Strategy # 5: Avoid Toxic People Altogether

Realize that you don't have to tolerate irrational behavior. Establish boundaries for your own physical safety and emotional health. Draw an invisible line in the sand and then will walk away when your boundaries are violated.

Stick to your convictions and do not relapse and go back into passive behavior. Intentionally remember the pain of the past with toxic people and avoid it for the future.

Strategy # 6: Use God's Wisdom

Develop a "bull-dog tenacity" to sidestep and not get involved with an abuser and become a victim of domestic violence and emotional and verbal abuse again.

THE VICTOR'S PRAYER

Heavenly Father,
Make Your presence known
to me each and every day.
Let me feel Your presence
as the God who is near
to the brokenhearted
and who saves the crushed in
spirit (see Psalm 34:18).
I need You, Lord,
to help me be the unique
and authentic person
You created me to be.
Thank You for answering my prayer.
In Jesus' name,
Amen!

From Victim to Victory

Ye shall know the truth, and the truth shall make you free. John 8:32, KJV

As the Lord was with Joseph
(Genesis chapters 37-50),
so has the Lord been with Jan!

POWER KEY #3

BE VERBAL (SAY SOMETHING)

In my distress, I called to the LORD;
I cried to my God for help.
From His Temple He heard my voice;
my cry came before Him, unto His ears.

Psalm 18:6

To move from victim to victory and recover from the trauma and drama of domestic abuse, one must be verbal. Tell somebody what's going on!

THE ART OF COMMUNICATION IN THE SANCTITY OF MARRIAGE

Marriage can be a joyous and sacred union between a man and women, when a loving couple is completely open and honest with each other. They can freely discuss and share their intimate secrets and confidences with each other without fear of being compromised. They are drawn together in a love designed by God, a love that is both physical and spiritual. They know each other better than any other person on the face of this planet because of their active and open communication skills. Between them, there is a sense of serenity and wholesomeness that keeps the communication channels open and freely flowing. They easily talk to and with each other about anything and everything.

However, when one of the two partners stops talking, becomes secretive, or becomes verbally abusive, that close marital relationship will break down and rapidly deteriorate. The marriage relationship then becomes toxic and dysfunctional. Those same words—secrets and confidences—previously revealed and shared in an atmosphere of love and openness, now may be used as weapons of mass destruction. Those same words are now used to assault and abuse the other partner. I know because that's precisely what happened to me.

What Is Verbal Abuse?

Verbal abuse is a kind of battering that doesn't leave evidence like bruises from a physical battering, but the negative effects can be far more damaging than physical abuse. Verbal abuse is a form of abusive behavior used with words by one partner. Verbal abuse is the systematic use of upsetting words intended to hurt, control, and dominate the victim. Toxic words can cause fear, intimidation, and humiliation that undermine the other partner's self-esteem and self-worth.

Some Examples of Verbal Abuse

Some examples of verbal abuse are:

- Attacking a person's identity
- Name-calling
- Insulting
- Yelling
- Accusing
- Backbiting
- Bullying
- Criticizing unjustly
- Shaming publicly
- Breaking promises
- Degrading
- Chronically complaining
- Lying
- Truth twisting
- Threatening
- Ridiculing

What Is Emotional Abuse?

Emotional abuse is the continuous use of negative behavior intended to control and hurt the victim. Emotional abuse wounds the spirit of the victim and is emotionally destructive.

SOME EXAMPLES OF EMOTIONAL ABUSE

Some example of emotional abuse are:

- Intimidating
- Degrading
- Ignoring
- Exploiting
- Isolating
- Discrediting
- Forgetting
- Labeling

WHAT ARE THE CONSEQUENCES OF VERBAL AND EMOTIONAL ABUSE?

The effects of verbal and emotional abuse for me included:

- Loss of self-worth
- Loss of hope
- Loss of self-respect
- Loss of happiness
- Loss of security
- Loss of positive self-perception
- Loss of inner peace

WHY DO VICTIMS OF DOMESTIC ABUSE KEEP SILENT?

The reasons victims of domestic abuse remain silent and

Be Verbal (Say Something)

do not tell others what is going on in their lives vary from victim to victim, but the list can be simplified and categorized as follows:

- Fear of calling attention to their problem
- Embarrassment and/or shame
- Fear that no one will believe them
- Fear of secrets revealed and consequences enacted
- Fear of being misunderstood
- Fear of being judged and criticized

What Happens When We Suffer in Silence?

The consequences of not telling someone about domestic abuse may be catastrophic. By remaining silent about the problem, this is what happens:

- The enemy wins.
- God's power is untapped and unused, and He does not get the glory.
- The longer the abuse goes on, the less likely it is that the victim will receive the necessary help.
- The abuse plays into the hands of the abuser, who is ultimately not exposed or held accountable and, therefore, continues the offense without penalty.
- The silence highlights the isolation of the victim.
- Keeping silent intensifies the negative thought process and

delays or prevents positive solutions to the problem.
- Keeping silent delays or impedes the healing process.
- Not verbalizing the toxicity of domestic abuse perpetuates the stigma of the experience.
- Remaining silent keeps one from being true to oneself.

You owe it to yourself to acknowledge what is going on and find the courage to ask for help. Reach out to someone you trust. Tell somebody, but not everybody. Speak up, but use wisdom!

Why Did I Refuse to Tell Anyone about My Abuse?

I realize that in today's generation, with reality TV and social media, people say anything and everything. They are like unplugged refrigerators; they can't keep anything. It is rare for the average person to keep anything to themselves even for a day, let alone for forty-two years. I am sure the fact that I remained silent sounds incredible to modern generations, but there are four valid reasons I remained silent about my years of abuse, never even telling my own parents:

1. Generational Conditioning

In my generation, we were taught to keep our mouths closed and our thoughts to ourselves. I grew up when it was proper for children to be seen and not heard. We were instructed to be

Be Verbal (Say Something)

quiet, especially in the presence of adults. I grew up quiet and restrained. Even in my early adult years, I continued the same conduct. In other words, I learned how to keep my business to myself. Therefore, I just never confided in friends or spoke candidly about what was going on in my life.

2. A Non-Communicative Relationship with My Husband

After I had married Husband Number One, I discovered that he was an extremely private person who rarely openly communicated much about anything. Initially, I had thought that his quiet nature was what had attracted me to him. I saw him as the strong, silent type that I had admired in movies. I soon learned, however, that a talkative and more open man would have been a better match for me.

3. Too Embarrassed and Ashamed

Once I found myself in a violent and painful marital relationship, I was too embarrassed and ashamed to share my experiences with others. After all, what would they think of me? What would they tell others about me? Just the thought of being the topic of gossip was mortifying, so I chose to lie in my proverbial "hard bed."

4. Too Fearful and Stressed Out

Vincent's terrorizing behavior had kept me from making any

close friends locally. In fact, I didn't even know my neighbors. His hostility and lack of socialization had kept me isolated from others. At times, the atmosphere in our home was so scary and horrible that stress engulfed me. I would break out in hives, and my hair would fall out in clumps when I combed it. I was a total mess—physically, emotionally, and spiritually. Still, I didn't share with anyone the Hell I was experiencing.

Sure, I attended my local church every week, went to work every day, and interacted with many people, but no one suspected my secret.

WHAT ARE SOME RED FLAGS THAT INDICATE A PERSON IS A VERBAL ABUSER?

Unfortunately, I did not recognize the red flags of domestic violence. Perhaps you, too, are a victim and simply don't realize it. Consider the following danger signs for yourself:

❑ Your partner threatens you and is violent toward you and the children.
❑ You find yourself making excuses for or minimizing the seriousness of your spouse's behavior.
❑ You frequently feel controlled and manipulated by your spouse.
❑ Sometimes you feel trapped, helpless, alone, and isolated, and you don't know which way to turn.

Be Verbal (Say Something)

- ❏ You often blame yourself for your partner's abuse, taking personal responsibility for the mistreatment.
- ❏ Your partner says *you* are the cause of the problems, and you believe it.
- ❏ You often fear going home.
- ❏ You are embarrassed or humiliated by your partner to control your behavior, especially in public.
- ❏ You are limited in your freedom (such as going shopping, to the hairdresser, etc.). You are timed and told to come straight home within a set period.
- ❏ You lie to hide your partner's real behavior. (You say, for example, that you fell down the stairs; in actuality, you were pushed).

YOU COULD BE A VICTIM IF YOU CHECKED OFF ONE OR MORE OF THESE "RED FLAGS!"

To move from victim to victory and recover from the trauma and drama of domestic abuse, it is necessary to talk about it; tell someone!

BUT ... I DID TRY EARLY ON TO VERBALIZE MY EXPERIENCES WITH DOMESTIC ABUSE

At the beginning of my marriage, I did try to tell others about my domestic abuse (unsuccessfully) on three separate occasions: 1). A police officer. 2). A group of elderly women at a church and 3). My own pastor.

From Victim to Victory

#1. I Tried to Tell a Police Officer about Being Physically Abused.[1]

One Saturday afternoon, Vincent went into one of his foul moods, and before I knew what was happening, we were arguing, hitting, yelling, and banging doors so loudly in our tiny one-bedroom apartment that I suppose the entire neighborhood could hear us. To this day I don't know which neighbor it was who called the police, but I thank God for that neighbor, who probably feared for my safety and made the call.

We lived in the 1960s, before 911 service was established, but soon I heard a loud knock at the front door, and a deep, authoritative male voice said, "Open up! This is the police!"

At that point, my heart leaped for joy! I felt that I was finally going to get some protection and some justice. I was ready to open up about everything Husband Number One had been doing to me. I felt that this defender of the rights of others would listen patiently to me and come up with solutions to my problems. But that was not what happened.

Vincent answered the door before I could get there and gave the officer "his side of the story." The young and inexperienced police officer believed every word Vincent told him and never considered asking for my version of the truth. Naturally, I was

---
1. See *Testimony of a Kept Woman, pp. 67-71*

Be Verbal (Say Something)

shocked and disturbed beyond words. I was so upset that I started protesting about the unfairness and injustice of it all … until the unthinkable happened. The police officer slowly turned back around, looked me squarely in the face, and told me in no uncertain terms: "Lady, if you don't lower your voice and get control of yourself in a hurry, I'm going to have to arrest you and take you downtown for disturbing the peace!" That day I realized I could never depend on "the law" to assist me.

#2. I Tried to Tell the Elderly Women at a Storefront Church[2]

One evening, I dashed from our apartment when Vincent's explosive temper had erupted. I had to get away from him. I ended up stumbling into a storefront church where some older ladies were meeting. My heart leaped for joy when I saw them, for surely I could find solace with this group. It was as if my "heavenly guardian angels" had guided me to a place where I could safely open up about what I was enduring with my aggressive husband. Those elderly missionaries, those sweet and loving grandmotherly figures would surely listen, encourage me with words of wisdom, and put their arms around me for support and sympathy. But none of that occurred.

Instead, those older women looked at me with contempt, folded their arms in defiance, and gave the cold stare of ridicule,

---
2. See *Testimony of a Kept Woman*, pp. 62-65

condemnation, and rejection. Their message was clear: "Young lady, you got yourself into this mess! Don't think that we are going to get involved in your drama! We don't want to hear anything you have to say! Now, get out of here!"

Wow! That experience marked me for life. The cold and indifferent response of those older church women shocked me so badly that I decided to return to my tiny apartment and deal with my bipolar and violent husband on my own. If "spiritually mature older church women" wouldn't support and/or offer assistance to a troubled young woman who was experiencing severe problems with domestic violence, then surely no one else would.

#3. I Tried to Tell My Own Pastor About My Domestic Violence.[3]

In 1964, when I was finally at my wit's end, I decided to go to my pastor for help. He was an excellent pastor–wise, spiritual, warm, and caring—but he was utterly ignorant of the seriousness of my situation. He patronized me and suggested that I be more submissive to my husband. In his way of thinking, I was the problem, and if I would just stop aggravating my husband, listen to him, and be more caring about his needs, the problem would disappear. Well, for me, that was it. After three strikeouts, I resolved never again to communicate my problem

---
3. See *Testimony of a Kept Woman*, pp. 65-67

to others. Looking to others for help had proved futile. I was determined to pray to God and let Him direct my path. After all, I could tell Him anything, and He would never condemn me or make me feel that the problem was solely mine.

In my distress, I cried unto the Lord, and he heard me.
Psalm 120:1, KJV

The Problem of Silence in Domestic Abuse

Kerby Anderson of Probe Ministries says that verbal abuse is often more difficult to see since there are rarely any visible scars unless physical abuse has taken place. Verbal abuse is usually less obvious just because the damage may always take place in private. The victim of verbal abuse lives in a gradually more confusing realm. In public, the victim is with one person, while, in private, the abuser may become an entirely different person.

Our country and perhaps the world has a severe problem of ignoring the pervasive problem of domestic abuse. The problem has not fully come into the consciousness and conversation of health service workers, religious leaders, or even the average citizen, for that matter. And why is that? I believe it is because the subject is still taboo, and victims are hesitant to reveal their struggles for fear of being ridiculed.

Beginning on January 1, 2017, salon workers in Illinois were to receive domestic violence training. A new law was signed

From Victim to Victory

by Bruce Rauner, Govenor of Illinois from 2015 to 2019. Through House Bill 4264, amending the Barber, Cosmetology, Esthetics, Hair Braiding and Nail Technology Act of 1985, licensed beauty professionals are now required to take a course in domestic abuse and sexual assault education to identify signs of domestic abuse and sexual assault. This was a first-of-its-kind law provided for hair salon employees throughout the state. It is said that salon customers often feel comfortable sharing personal information they might not otherwise disclose to friends or family.[4] This is a good start.

WHY IS IT SO IMPORTANT TO TALK ABOUT VERBAL ABUSE?

We must talk about verbal abuse because it thrives in secrecy and silence. The abuser's objective over the victim is two-fold:

1. To maintain power and control
2. To achieve authority and power by any means necessary, including but not limited to the following:
- Physical violence
- Psychological manipulation
- Emotional and verbal abuse

WHAT ARE THE MOTIVES OF THE VERBAL ABUSER?

The motives of the verbal abuser are:

---

4. http://www.nwherald.com/2016/11/18/new-law-requires-salon-workers-in-illinois-ge

Be Verbal (Say Something)

- To embarrass
- To manipulate
- To criticize
- To threaten
- To intimidate
- To pressure
- To terrorize
- To silence
- To control

WHY WE MUST SPEAK UP AND SPEAK OUT ABOUT VERBAL AND EMOTIONAL ABUSE

Both Vincent and Harry systematically worked to diminish me as a person. Between them, those two abusers wounded me emotionally and psychologically. They denied who I was as a person, and they told me that my feelings and my perception of reality were mistaken.

According to Patricia Evans in her excellent book, *The Verbally Abusive Relationship*,[5] not all verbal abuse becomes physical, but virtually all physical abuse is preceded by verbal abuse.

Verbal abuse, also called verbal battering, is a particularly insidious form of domestic violence. Although it does not leave outward scars, it is calculated to assassinate the character and kill the inner person with cruelty, belittling, put-downs,

5. Avon, MA: Adams Media, 2010

shaming, name calling, intimidation, rage, silence, criticizing, blaming, twisting the truth, the rewriting of history, and strategic "forgetting." All types of verbal abuse are designed to inflict injury. Sticks and stones may break our bones, but words can break our spirits and our hearts.

Questions:

1. In reading the types of verbal abuse, which have you experienced?
2. How does each category of verbal abuse give the abuser power and control?
3. How does each type of verbal abuse attempt to silence the victim and make her more powerless?[6]

WHAT DOES THE BIBLE SAY ABOUT VERBAL AND EMOTIONAL ABUSE?

The Word of God has plenty to say about verbal abuse. The Bible addresses victims of verbal abuse because their experience provokes a particular kind of agony. It is true that verbal and emotional abuse do not leave physical bruises on the body, but, with me, the verbal and emotional abuse were just as painful (or even more so), and the recovery time was also much longer.

> *Death and life are in the power of the tongue,*
> *and those who love it will eat its fruits.*
>
> Proverbs 18:21, ESV

---
6. http://www.abigails.org/Workbook.pdf pp. 26-27

Be Verbal (Say Something)

I tell you, on the day of judgment people will give account for every careless word they speak, for by your words you will be justified, and by your words you will be condemned. Matthew 12:36-37, ESV

*The LORD is near to the brokenhearted
  and saves the crushed in spirit.* Psalm 34:18, ESV

Husbands, love your wives, and do not be harsh with them. Colossians 3:19, ESV

Let no corrupting talk come out of your mouths, but only such as is good for building up, as fits the occasion, that it may give grace to those who hear.
Ephesians 4:29, ESV

Let all bitterness and wrath and anger and clamor and slander be put away from you, along with all malice.
Ephesians 4:31, ESV

ABUSERS DENY VERBAL AND EMOTIONAL ABUSE

Sadly, verbal abusers often deny the abuse and seek to blame the victim for it. Abusers tend to escalate their attacks when confronted, in an attempt to reassert power and control. Both of my former husbands denied the abuse. They said that I was "too sensitive," or I "just couldn't take a joke." In short, they blamed me, the victim.

From Victim to Victory

Without any evidence of physical bruises, I doubted that I had been abused, and yet I knew that I had. Emotional and verbal abuse can cause confusion, doubt, and frustration in the victim. Although it did not work for me, it might be possible to get assistance from a professional counselor who specializes in domestic violence and is trained to help the abuser to see the pattern of abuse and its effects. However, no one can force an abuser to change.[7]

TO GOD BE THE GLORY!

---

7. http://www.abigails.org/Workbook.pdf pp. 28-29

— An Important Question —

So, how do you recover from the trauma and drama of domestic abuse and become verbal?

Strategies

Strategy # 1: Open Your Mouth and Tell Someone You Trust about the Abuse

Share your story with a friend of confidence, and seek help that way. Verbalizing your issues can be therapeutic and contributes to promoting mental, social, physical and spiritual healing.

Strategy # 2: Stop Condemning Yourself. You Are Not Weak

If you have a physical problem, you will visit a physician. Turning to a professional to help cope with abuse is not a sign of weakness. To the contrary, it shows great strength.

Strategy # 3: There is No Stigma in Being a Former Victim

Pride is ugly, and God hates it. Uncover the devil's tricks by telling it! Refuse to sit silently on the sidelines, hoping that the problem will somehow magically resolve itself.

Strategy # 4: Stop Your Denial. Face the Truth and Deal with It

Jesus said, *"The truth will set you free."* And it's true, I am free indeed!

> *The thief cometh not, but for to steal, and to kill, and to destroy: I am come that they might have life, and that they might have it more abundantly.*
> John 10:10, KJV

Try to get help and deal openly and honestly with your abusive partner.

Strategy # 5: Use the Scriptures to Master Fear and Condemnation

The following list of verses are helpful to spiritually strengthen you as you cry out to the Lord and others:

> *This poor man cried, and the LORD heard him and saved him out of all his troubles.* Psalm 34:6, KJV

> *From the end of the earth I call to You when my heart is faint; lead me to the rock that is higher than I.* Psalm 61:2, NRS

Oh give thanks to the Lord, call upon His name;
Make known His deeds among the peoples.
Psalm 105:1, NASB

Because He has inclined His ear to me.
Therefore I shall call upon Him as long as I live.
Psalm 116:2, NASB

Call upon Me in the day of trouble;
I shall rescue you, and you will honor Me.
Psalm 50:15, NASB

I will call upon the Lord, who is worthy to be praised;
So, shall I be saved from my enemies.
2 Samuel 22:4, NKJV

The Victor's Prayer

Heavenly Father,
You made my mouth.
You want me to call on You
during my time of need.
You want me to praise You
at all times.
Incline Your ear to my cry.
Listen and answer my prayer
each time I call.
Thank You for being my God.
In Jesus name, I pray,
Amen!

From Victim to Victory

Ye shall know the truth, and the truth shall make you free.   John 8:32, KJV

As the Lord was with Joseph
(Genesis Chapters 37-50),
so has the Lord been with Jan!

Power Key #4

Be Forgetful (Intentionally)

Brothers and sisters, I do not consider that I have made it my own yet; but one thing I do: forgetting what lies behind and reaching forward to what lies ahead, I press on toward the goal to win the [heavenly] prize of the upward call of God in Christ Jesus.

Philippians 3:13-14, AMP

To move from victim to victory and recover from the trauma and drama of domestic abuse, one must become intentionally forgetful.

A Good Memory is Commendable

It is almost a universal truth that everyone desires to have a good memory. Having the ability to recall facts, give information quickly, and reminiscence from the past is considered to be intelligent and significantly beneficial. All of us have struggled to remember a particular event or to be able to articulate the right words at the right time. Surely most of us have become embarrassed at one time or another when we couldn't immediately recollect names, dates, or details. That is a normal fact of life. We just acknowledge our human frailties and laughingly agree that perhaps we are just having a senior moment. But no one wants to experience dementia, nor even a mild case of cognitive impairment, especially as we grow older. One of life's great tragedies is the loss of memory.

SOME THINGS SHOULD BE FORGOTTEN

But, there are things that we *should* forget. I am now physically, mentally, and emotionally free from domestic violence and abuse, but it would not take much for me to relive the misery of the past. All it would take is to hear a negative word, smell a particular scent, or listen to a song from my distant past, or just think about an incident that has some connection to my previous life, and I could be immediately transported back to:

- Times when I was petrified with fear whenever my husband became irritable, angry, or upset about one thing or another.

- Times when his mood would fluctuate between highs and lows, and his actions would become physically violent, erratic, and unpredictable.

Be Forgetful (Intentionally)

- Times when things went wrong for him, and he would say it was my fault and take out his frustrations on me by either using the silent treatment (that could go on for days, weeks, or even months), and then vent his frustrations on me by yelling and cursing at the top of his lungs.

- Times when he would get upset about something that happened at work, but would wait until he came home to burst into an angry fit over it.

- Times when he would go into my closet, snatching down my best clothes from hangers, throwing them on the floor, and systematically destroying them with scissors or ripping them to pieces one by one with his bare hands.

- Times when he would explode with anger for seemingly no reason at all and then begin calling me every dirty name in the book, telling me how stupid I was, and yelling how I could never do anything right.

- The time when I found out, at a church business meeting, that the very same women who had visited me in my home and acted as if they were my friends had been the mistresses of my husband, their pastor.

From Victim to Victory

- The time when I stepped to the microphone in a packed sanctuary and voiced my support for my cheating husband and my disdain for the women who had taken advantage of me and his blindness.

- Times when I would drive down the highway with tears blinding my eyes and hear Satan whisper to me, "Why don't you just press down hard on the accelerator, turn the wheel slightly left, and go into the lane of that oncoming eighteen-wheeler. You'd be out of your misery, and it would look like an accident. Nobody would ever suspect that you did it on purpose."

- The time when the man I loved and married more than twenty-two years earlier coldly spoke words that changed my life forever. He said, "I'm sorry, but this marriage is over. I don't love you anymore, and I am getting a divorce."

- The time when I answered the front door of my home and the uniformed officer asked my name, pulled an envelope from his inside coat pocket, placed it in my hand, and said, "Your husband has sued you for divorce."

Yes, having a good memory could be a good thing. Memories connected me to the past. But I needed to find a way to pick and choose the memories that would encourage me to move forward and upward. I needed to find a way to reject and forget those devastating memories that kept flooding back into my mind, sending me hurling into a sea of depression or sadness.

It was so quick and easy. All it would take was just one incident, and instantaneously, the bad memories would propel me back into the Hell and torment of yesteryears. The past was still inside my head. I had to find a way to stop remembering.

Selective Amnesia Can be Beneficial

There were times when I chose to exercise selective amnesia. When I felt myself slipping into a negative mood or becoming sad and depressed, I intentionally decided to take control of my thoughts and forget the past. I did not confuse selecting what to forget with mindlessly forgetting everything. That would neither be possible nor healthy. It was important to remember certain negative aspects of the past, so that I would not repeat them. However, it was also imperative for me not to focus on the past hurts and pain, especially those thoughts that would lead me into a state of depression and sadness.

One of my favorite Pauline letters is Philippians. I especially love chapter 3. The apostle Paul had some bad experiences he needed to forget to be an ambassador of Christ. He had done some awful things in his past. Believe it or not, he was an abusive bully who had persecuted Christians and even killed some in the early part of his unsaved life.

When Paul came to the knowledge of the truth (see Acts 9), he was devastated about his past. He knew that he needed to let go of his negative thoughts about himself because they were sure to hinder his progress and make him ineffective for Christ and even emotionally ill. So, what did the apostle Paul do? He was wise. He intentionally forgot the past. He said:

> *No, dear brothers and sisters, I have not achieved it, but I focus on this one thing: Forgetting the past and looking forward to what lies ahead.* Philippians 3:13, NLT

Yes, Paul purposely forgot the bad things he had done. He had to put those things behind him. He went on to say:

> I press on to reach the end of the race and receive the heavenly prize for which God, through Christ Jesus, is calling us. Philippians 3:14, NLT

Paul let me know that his conduct was not regulated nor influenced by what others thought of him. His only consideration was his calling in Christ. He had no time to loiter or trifle because God had a plan and a purpose for his life.

Be Forgetful (Intentionally)

These words from Paul were electrifying to me because he had done some seriously offensive things in his past. This man we consider to be a saint today had a past for which he was not proud. It was evidently that he had lots of regrets. However, he was able to put all his negative past behind him and move on to the assignment God had given him.

How Did Paul Accomplish this Seemingly Impossible Task?

I learned that Paul used the strategy of selective amnesia. He forgot his past and turned his back on it. He intentionally refused to remember anything that would hinder his progress. He let it go and moved forward to what was ahead.

It was the apostle Paul who taught me that nothing is impossible with Christ. I thought to myself, "If Paul could achieve this monumental task with Jesus, then so can I." I was determined to succeed. The realization of God's *agape* love for me began to resonate in my heart and mind. Slowly but surely, God's love empowered and transformed me.

The apostle Paul also taught me that anything that disrupted my peace and tranquility needed to be placed in the far recesses of my mind. When I intentionally chose to forget the negatives of my past, I rediscovered my purpose, and God recycled my life. Oddly enough, I became better instead of bitter and moved from victim to victory.

Now I was willing to do whatever it took for God to restore my life. I was determined to hang in there and keep hope alive. I would not let my past brokenness and disappointments affect my perception of the future the Lord was sending my way. I refused to let my past hurts teach me to be cynical. I chose to forget the pain that would cause me to put up my guard and make fists instead of opening up my hands, arms, and heart to all the good the Lord had in store for me.

REFOCUSING AND RESTRUCTURING THE MIND

I questioned myself, "Is it possible to forget the past? And is forgetting the past even biblical?" I pondered this critical issue and did some biblical research and found answers to my questions. Yes, God does want us to forget some things and not dwell on hurtful thoughts. As a matter of fact, the Holy Spirit inspired the apostle to write a scripture that helped me reprogram my negative thinking and focus on the positive:

> *Finally, brothers, whatever is true, whatever is honorable, whatever is just, whatever is pure, whatever is lovely, whatever is commendable, if there is any excellence, if there is anything worthy of praise, think about these things.*   Philippians 4:8, NASB

Through the apostle Paul, God was telling me to forget what was weighing me down and causing me to become depressed and sad. He had given me the ability to choose my thoughts. I needed to dwell on what was good. He had empowered and enabled me to learn from my past mistakes. I chose to focus on the good and forget the rest. Now, all I had to do was reach out and take hold of His divine spiritual tool of forgetfulness.

There Is a Time to Forget

I'm so glad that God inspired King Solomon to write Ecclesiastes 3. It says exactly what I needed to know:

> *To everything there is a season, and a time to every purpose under the heaven:*
> *A time to be born, and a time to die; a time to plant, and a time to pluck up that which is planted; a time to kill, and a time to heal; a time to break down, and a time to build up; a time to weep, and a time to laugh; a time to mourn, and a time to dance; a time to cast away stones, and a time to gather stones together; a time to embrace, and a time to refrain from embracing; a time to get, and a time to lose; a time to keep, and a time to cast away; a time to rend, and a time to sew; a time to keep silence, and a time to speak; a time to love, and a time to hate; a time of war, and a time of peace.*   Ecclesiastes 3:1-8, KJV

The Bible says that King Solomon was the wisest man who ever lived (see 1 Kings 4:30). I am so glad the Lord said through

Solomon that there's a time to do everything—even a time to forget the past.

Even God Forgets

Jesus paid for sin once, and His payment was complete. Several passages in the Bible indicate that God forgets and does not remember our sins:

> *I, even I, am he who blots out your transgressions, for my own sake, and remembers your sins no more.* Isaiah 43:25

> *For by one sacrifice, he has made perfect forever those who are being made holy. Their sins and lawless acts I will remember no more.* Hebrews 10:14 and 17

> *So now there is no condemnation for those who belong to Christ Jesus.* Romans 8:1, NLT

A Transformed Mind Is Not Automatic

This new-found truth was not easy or quick for me to implement. It took time for me to discover the truth about myself. It took time for me to restore my self-esteem and self-worth:

> *Don't copy the behavior and customs of this world, but let God transform you into a new person by changing*

Be Forgetful (Intentionally)

the way you think. Then you will learn to know God's will for you, which is good and pleasing and perfect.
Romans 12:2, NLT

Now to Him who is able to do exceedingly abundantly above all that we ask or think, according to the power that works in us ... .   Ephesians 3:20, NKJV

I focus on this one thing: Forgetting the past and looking forward to what lies ahead.   Philippians 3:13, NLT

The transformation of my mind began when I rediscovered who I was in Christ. It took time for me to be enabled and empowered to forget the past and believe in the future God had in store for me, but it did happen. I am now free from the excess baggage of my past. With prayer and consistent reading of the Scriptures, I continued to forget the negative and moved forward to the positive future the Lord Jesus had in store for me.

TO GOD BE THE GLORY!

—— AN IMPORTANT QUESTION ——

So, how do you intentionally forget the mental anguish of your negative experiences and move from victim to victory?

Strategies

Strategy # 1: Deliberately Choose Selective Amnesia to Forget the Negative

Like Paul, you can forget what is behind and *press on toward the goal to win the prize for which God has called you heavenward in Christ Jesus* (see Philippians 3:13).

Practicing selective amnesia is a healthy way to forget your negative past. Forgetting the past is not easy and will not happen overnight.

Be patient with yourself. It will take some time to master selecting your thoughts. Retraining your mind not to revert to negative thinking is not automatic. It will take time to discover the truth that you can purposely choose your thoughts.

Read the Word, pray and practice selective amnesia. Slowly, you will be transformed into a new way of thinking.

Strategy # 2: Intentionally Reprogram Your Mind to Remember the Good

Whatever is true, whatever is noble, whatever is right, whatever is pure, whatever is lovely, whatever is admirable-if anything is excellent or praiseworthy—think about such things. Philippians 4:8

Most people automatically dwell on the negatives of their current situation. But it is possible to intentionally reprogram your mind. You may have become accustomed to seeing the proverbial "hole" and not the donut. The best thing parents can spend on their children is time. It doesn't take any effort to focus on the negative, but it will take some real energy, force, and power to redirect your thoughts to the positive.

Choose to remember the good and not the bad. It might be difficult at first, but it is possible to continue the process. Although you have experienced some horrific events, it was not all bad. There were some hilarious episodes. With prayer, consistency, and sheer will power, begin to change how you think. Time is short, and life is precious

Strategy # 3: Intentionally Choose God's Prescriptive Scriptures

Jesus Christ is the Master Physician Himself. His Words have healing properties that are universal and unlimited. The best thing about using this prescription is that it is free. There is never a monetary charge for the best medicine in the world, and it is available for the taking. You have no medical bills, and you don't have to be afraid of overdosing on this medication:

> *This [trusting in the Lord] will bring health to your body and <u>nourishment</u> to your bones.*
> Proverbs 3:8

God has a plan for healing and moving forward, reading the Scriptures and praying daily:

> *I alone am the one who is going to wipe away your rebellious actions for my sake. I will not remember your sins anymore.* Isaiah 43:25, GW

God sees all our sins—past, present, and future—and still He says:

> *Their [your] sins and lawless acts I will remember no more.*   Hebrews 10:17

You must do the same.

Strategy # 4: Intentionally Pray to Soothe and Relax Your Mind

Reading and praying the Psalms in the Bible can soothe and relax your mind when you are troubled or stressed. Psalm 8 helps to remind you just how special you are. Practice personalizing the Scriptures (God's love letters to you) so that they will relate and benefit you in a specific way:

> O Lord, our Lord,
> How majestic and glorious and excellent is Your name in all the earth!
> When I see and consider Your heavens, the work of Your fingers,
> The moon and the stars, which You have established,
> What is a man [who am I] that You are mindful of [me],
> And the [daughter] of the [earthborn] man that You care for [me]?

Strategies

*Yet You have made [me] a little lower than God,
And You have crowned [me] with glory and honor.
You made [me] to have dominion over the works of Your hands;
You have put all things under [my] feet,
O LORD, our Lord,
How majestic and glorious and excellent is Your name in all the earth!* Psalm 8:1, 3-6 and 9, AMP

What a beautiful psalm! Without prayer and the Scriptures, you will never completely become whole and perfectly functioning in this dark world. This is a spiritual battle that you will win if you fight the good fight of faith. Paul wrote:

Brethren, I count not myself to have apprehended: but this one thing I do, forgetting those things which are behind, and reaching forth unto those things which are before, I press toward the mark of the high calling of God in Christ Jesus.
Philippians 3:13-14, KJV

TO GOD BE THE GLORY!

From Victim to Victory

THE VICTOR'S PRAYER

Heavenly Father,
Please make Your presence known
to me each and every day.
Let me remember that You are near to
the brokenhearted and You save the
crushed in spirit (see Psalm 34:18).
Lord, I feel crushed and broken. I
need You. Please help me.
In Your name, Father God, I speak healing and restoration for myself and everyone
who has been wounded by an abuser.
Thank You for healing and
binding my wounds, Lord!
In Jesus' name, I pray,
Amen!

Be Forgetful (Intentionally)

Ye shall know the truth, and the truth shall make you free.   John 8:32, KJV

As the Lord was with Joseph
(Genesis Chapters 37-50),
so has the Lord been with Jan!

Power Key #5

Be Vigilant (Not Gaslighted!)

*Watch over your heart with all diligence,
For from it flow the springs of life.* Proverbs 4:23, AMP

To move from victim to victory and recover from the trauma and drama of domestic abuse, one must be vigilant.

What is Vigilance?

Merriam-Webster.com defines *vigilance* as "the action or state of keeping careful watch for possible danger or difficulties; the quality or state of being wakeful and alert." *Vigilance* is "the state of continually being watchful of potential risks or threats." I was not vigilant, but the Lord was still with me.

There is a Correlation Between Low Self-Esteem and Gaslighting

Low self-esteem and low self-worth kept me locked into a

dysfunctional and physically violent and doomed marriage for nearly twenty traumatic years with Husband Number One. Finally, I came to my senses and divorced Vincent. Sometime later, I met a smooth-talking, slow-walking, charming and charismatic young man named Harry. He was fantastic. Although Harry was blind from birth, he had 20/20 vision compared to me. I was desperately needy and pitiful, and it was easy for Harry to sense my emotional state.

I had been starving for attention and affection for years. Harry immediately picked up on my vulnerability and took advantage of this golden opportunity of finding his perfect victim. Sad, but true, even a blind man could see how blind I was. Because I had been going through life with my eyes wide shut, I was gullible, naïve and easily deceived.

> *One who is full loathes honey, but to one who is hungry everything bitter is sweet.*   Proverbs 27:7, ESV

Harry found me to be an easy target and the perfect candidate to become a victim to be manipulated and psychologically controlled by the mind game called gaslighting.

What is Gaslighting?

Gaslighting is a devious, sneaky, and insidious mind game. According to "Psychology Today," gaslighting is "a form of psychological abuse that manipulates the victim into doubting their memory, perception, and sanity." Gaslighting, at its core, is "a kind of emotional abuse that slowly eats away at the victim's self-esteem and ability to make sound judgments."

Robin Stern, Ph.D., a licensed psychoanalyst and author of *The Gaslight Effect,*[1] describes gaslighting as "a form of psychological abuse that manipulates a victim into doubting his or her memory and perceptions."

WHERE DID THE TERM "GASLIGHTING" AS AN ABUSE ORIGINATE?

The term gaslighting comes from the 1944 classic movie entitled "Gaslight." It starred Ingrid Bergman, playing the wife and victim. Charles Boyer played the role of the husband and villain. The husband would insidiously make gradual changes in a room by dimming the gas lights ever so slightly in their home. Whenever his wife commented on the dimness of the room, he would dismiss what she said and insist that nothing had changed. Over a period of time, he finally convinced her that there had to be something dreadfully wrong with her because she was only imagining those changes. In this way, he played serious psychological games with her mind.

---
1. en.wikipedia.org/wiki/gaslighting

Be Vigilant (Not Gaslighted!)

How Does Gaslighting Work?

Gaslighting operates in three distinct phases or periods. Although I was completely unaware of what was happening to me at the time, my horrific experience was systematically designed by Harry, who later became my second husband. I lived through these three different stages or phases:

1. The idealization phase
2. The devaluation phase
3. The discarding phase

1. The Idealization Phase

From the very first moment I met Harry, I was totally impressed and awed by him.[2] He was from Dallas, Texas and worked in the U.S. Department of Agriculture. I was still living and working as a school principal in Gary, Indiana. He had flown in to visit his mother and sister for a few weeks that summer. Harry was the exact opposite of Vincent. Vincent was much older than I. Harry was ten and a half years younger than I. Yes, I was a cougar!

Harry was a deacon in his church—smooth, gentle, personable, and complimentary. Because I had been starved and deprived of attention and affection for nearly twenty years, I was completely vulnerable and unsuspecting. Harry showered

---
2. See *Testimony of a Kept Woman*, pp. 125-130.

me with attention. He was loving, charming, exciting, and great fun. Having been previously ignored, physically abused, and belittled by Vincent, I craved attention. Harry, of course, picked up on this, recognized my need for attention, and immediately proceeded to sweep me off my feet. He appeared to admire everything about me and was proud of any and all my accomplishments, both personal and professional. He made me feel alive and full of joy. Life was exciting again. Even my two sons, Dexter and Lawrence, quickly bonded with Harry.

After two years of long distance dating, Harry and I eventually married, and he became Husband Number Two. Harry moved me and my two sons to Dallas. A year after we married, Harry and I adopted our ten-day-old baby daughter, and the five of us were one happy family ... or so I thought.

It was not long after we had begun to settle in as a family that Harry announced his call to the ministry. His desire was to attend seminary to enhance his biblical knowledge and become a better preacher and teacher of the Bible. But, because there were no biblical materials available in Braille at the time, his seminary professors encouraged me to attend his classes with him. And so, for the next ten years, Harry and I attended Bible colleges together. I assisted my husband with his biblical research, transcribed his assignments, wrote his term papers, and was his scribe for tests, which simplified the lesson preparations for his seminarian professors. Together, Harry and I worked and studied hard and completed all his courses. We did almost everything together.

I was now learning how to study the Bible that Vincent, Husband Number One, had driven me to read years earlier. Sometime later Harry became pastor of a prominent church in Texas. With Harry, Husband Number Two, I was happy, content, and fulfilled. But all of that was about to change.

2. The Devaluation Phase

After Harry graduated from seminary, received his doctorate in Biblical Studies and was excelling as an efficient pastor of a thriving church in Texas, I was no longer needed to help him "shine." He had achieved his goal, the status, and all the trappings of an up-and-coming, fruitful and prominent minister. His calendar was full of preaching invitations, and he was traveling all over the country holding city-wide revivals.

Needless to say, in time, our relationship slowly began to shift, and his feelings for me began to change. He became more and more elusive, and he started to ignore me and his children.

Naturally, this apparent change in Harry's feelings and treatment of me and the children was puzzling to me. I was simply clueless. I would ask him if I had done something that displeased him. He would say, "No, nothing different is going on." But, I knew better.

It's difficult to explain, but I felt as if I had somehow fallen from grace before his eyes. Over time, Harry's loving words slowly turned from compliments to criticism. The things I used to do for him that he loved and appreciated were no longer satisfying to him. As a matter of fact, no matter what I did for him, it was either not enough, or it was not right. He began to compare me to other women, both in and out of the church, and devalued me at every turn. I was totally confused and crushed by this bizarre and insensitive behavior.

I was totally unaware, but all the while, I had been a victim of gaslighting. By now, Harry's gaslighting was at its peak, and still, I was unaware of what was happening. Because I was clueless, I became increasingly stressed-out, unhappy, and depressed. I was distraught, confused, and bereaved over the soul-mate I had lost.

Herein was the paradox: the more I displayed my distress and concern over the deterioration of our relationship, the more empowered Harry became. In a word, Harry devalued me. He was merciless in his treatment of me:

- As his wife and mother of his children
- As a woman of God

- As First Lady of the church
- As a leader and teacher in the ministry

He used many different forms of attack on me.[3]

3. THE DISCARDING PHASE

By now, I was a total mess. The mind manipulation game of gaslighting was culminating in a nerve-wrecking crescendo. Harry had humiliated and devalued me as a person, and my self-esteem was at an all-time low. His gaslighting caused me to doubt my memories, my perceptions, and my personal judgments. And, all the while, I was losing my self-worth and credibility as a person.

Harry, on the other hand, seemed to be more thrilling than ever as a person. His self-confidence was now elevated, and he was becoming arrogant and prideful. He gloated and sneered in his power to reduce, demean, and degrade me at every turn.

Finally, came the last straw that broke the proverbial camel's back. Harry did the unthinkable. He sued me for divorce. Yes, he did! He traded me in for a younger woman. Even though he had no grounds, he divorced me and married a younger model of the many women with whom he had been having numerous affairs. One can only imagine the church scandal this caused.

---
3. See *Testimony of a Kept Woman*, pp. 165-170.

From Victim to Victory

I now felt that my life was over, and I was completely devastated. I even became suicidal.[4] What had started out as an ideal marriage to my soul-mate ended as a devastating, trauma-filled catastrophe. And, during the entire ordeal, Harry never showed any remorse toward me, his three children, or the members of the church who had loved him as their spiritual leader. He never displayed any sense of shame at his ungodly behavior. He seemed entirely oblivious to the fact that he was destroying many lives.

In effect, it was as if none of us mattered or existed in Harry's world. I will never understand how such a narcissist with untold arrogance could consider himself a "Man of God." What a paradox!

WHAT WERE MY REACTIONS TO GASLIGHTING?

During the torturous process of gaslighting, I drifted through three distinct emotional phases of mind control:

1. Disbelief
2. Defense
3. Depression[5]

#1. Disbelief: The traumatic effects of what had happened to me were so insidious that I almost lost all trust in my own

---

4. See *Testimony of a Kept Woman*, pp. 180-181)
5. See *Testimony of a Kept Woman*, pp.193-202

judgment and reality. After all, I had failed at marriage, not just once, but twice. "What's wrong with me?" I thought. I just couldn't do anything right. And I couldn't figure out what was happening to me.

#2. Defense: I felt defeated, and yet I still had enough self-will and stamina to fight and defend myself against losing my marriage. If Harry wanted to leave me for another woman, he would not find it easy. I put up a fight for my marriage because I loved him, and I had invested much into our relationship. I wasn't about to let him go without a struggle.

I know that sounds crazy after the way he had treated me,[6] but that's the way it had to be. Yes, he wanted to throw me off balance by creating self-doubt, anger, turmoil, and guilt. And his scheme nearly worked. The emotional damage did cause me to isolate myself later because of the embarrassment and humiliation I felt, but I prayed and persevered.

#3. Depression: Even though I persisted in trying to hold on to Harry and save my marriage, it didn't work. He still left. He discarded me like a used Kleenex®. Having served as First Lady and then having my dirty laundry aired in public was more than I could bear. By this time, I could hardly recognize myself.

---

6. See *Testimony of a Kept Woman*, pp. 179-183

I was becoming a shadow of my former self. I had been living in chaos—controlled physically and emotionally, sucked dry, and stripped of all dignity. Eventually, I slipped into a fog of depression. I also experienced Post Traumatic Stress Disorder (PTSD) and became only a shell of the person I had been.

Oh, but thanks be to the grace and mercy of the Lord Jesus Christ. Although I was down, one would have been entirely wrong to count me out. God created me in His image. I know this because the Bible tells me so (see Genesis 1:27). I had started out well, but the trauma and drama of domestic abuse nearly destroyed me. I would have to go through many deep valleys before I recovered and again reached my mountaintops.

I would not and did not remain a human wreck. Thankfully, the Providence of God enabled me to completely heal and recover.

To God be the Glory!

— AN IMPORTANT QUESTION —

So, how do you recover from "gaslighting," and move from victim to victory?

Strategies

STRATEGY #1 – PRAY FOR THE SPIRIT OF VIGILANCE

Gaslighting is spiritual warfare (see Ephesians 6:10-18). It is a grave and deadly battle of the mind. To become a whole person again, you will need an entirely different mindset.

> *And this I pray, that your love may abound still more and more in real knowledge and all discernment, so that you may approve the things that are excellent, to be sincere and blameless until the day of Christ.*
> Philippians 1:9-10, NKJV

> *Whoever is wise, let him understand these things; whoever is discerning, let him know them; for the ways of the LORD are right, and the upright walk in them, but transgressors stumble in them.*
> Hosea 14:9, RSV

Start a regimen of daily prayers and reading the book of Proverbs during the daytime and other scriptures at night. Your healing will be more supernatural than natural. Continue to read the book of Proverbs in the mornings because it's short and to the point.

Strategies

The book of Proverbs also reads like a monthly calendar. There are 31 chapters and 31 days in a month, so that is one chapter for each day of the month (you don't have to read the entire chapter for it to be effective).

Continue to regularly read scriptures on your computer, cell phone, iPad, and, of course, from your physical Bible. Listen to your audio Bible whenever you are driving in your car. In this way, saturate yourself with the Word of God for power and enlightenment.

These scriptures saved my life when the enemy tried to destroy me through bouts of depression and thoughts of suicide, when I had fallen to my lowest point.[7] Be convinced that it is out of your pain and spiritual poverty that God will produce your eternal purpose and complete His divine plan for your life.

Strategy #2: Admit Your Gullibility

Emotional and verbal abuse may have been going on for some time before you realized you were

---
7. See *Testimony of a Kept Woman,* pp. 180-181

a victim. Abusers are masterful and have perfected their tactics to keep themselves in control and their victims powerless. Become aware of the various forms of abuse being used against you, and begin to face the reality of your victimization. Only then will the process of healing start for you.

Once your eyes are opened to the tactical methods of your abusers, you will be able to move on toward victory.

> *A wise man will hear and will increase learning,*
> *And a man of understanding will attain wise counsel.*   Proverbs 1:5, NKJV

Educate yourself about emotional abuse by reading informative materials, joining groups that help to enhance your mental health, and expanding your experiences. Get involved in Bible studies, memorize scripture that uplifts your self-worth and increases your faith.

Trust in the Lord and learn to lean on the Holy Spirit to guide you. No matter how smart or intellectually brilliant you are, you are no match for the wiles of the devil. You need supernatural power to

Strategies

spiritually, emotionally, and physically overcome.

Don't isolate yourself. Stay connected to family, good friends, and members of your local church. This will be crucial for your healing and restoration.

Ignorance of psychological mind games and what's happening in spiritual warfare is not an option for today's Christian. The enemy wants you to remain isolated and aloof from others because he thrives on silence and secrecy.

Strategy # 3: Learn from Your Mistakes and Move On (see James 1:5).

Admit that you have made many mistakes. You are not alone. We have all failed at one time or another. The questions is: "How should you respond?"

Be honest and admit the truth. Don't get depressed and give up! Don't ignore your mistakes but learn from them. Lift up your eyes to the hills and trust in the Lord to give you another chance.

Our God is the God of the second chance ... the third chance ... and the fourth chance. Strive to be transformed by the renewing of your mind (see Romans 12:2).

Strategy # 4: Recognize Your Power in Christ Jesus

The greatest problem with domestic abuse is that it is more of a spiritual problem than a personal problem. Therefore, the solution must be approached spiritually if you are completely recover and heal.

Begin to place a high premium on yourself as the temple of the Living God and take care of yourself. Make yourself a top priority. The enemy wants to discourage and destroy you, but God will enable you to overcome, if you lean and depend on Him.

> *Put on the whole armor of God, that you may be able to stand against the wiles of the devil. For we do not wrestle against flesh and blood, but against principalities, against powers, against the rulers of the darkness of this age, against spiritual host of wickedness in the heavenly places.*
>
> Ephesians 6:11-12, NKJV

The Lord will teach you how to uncover your true authentic self by beginning to love yourself as Christ loves you. His *agape* love will strengthen and enable you to do things you could not otherwise do.

Read and study Psalm 139:14-18, a Psalm of David. It will help you realize who you are in Christ:

> *I praise you because I am fearfully and wonderfully made;*
> *your works are wonderful,*
> *I know that full well.*
> *My frame was not hidden from you*
> *when I was made in the secret place,*
> *when I was woven together in the depths*
> *of the earth,*
> *Your eyes saw my unformed body;*
> *all the days ordained for me were written*
> *in your book*
> *before one of them came to be.*
> *How precious to me are your thoughts, God!*
> *How vast is the sum of them!*
> *Were I to count them,*
> *they would outnumber the grains of sand—*
> *when I awake, I am still with you.*

Domestic violence and emotional and verbal abuse are spiritual problems, and it will take supernatural solutions to enable you to recover and heal from the devastation and damage done to your soul. Learn to lean and depend on the power and strength of God through the Holy Spirit for your victory.

Strategy #5: Set-Up Boundaries and Stick to Them

Realize that you are not the cause of the previous or present abuse problems, even though your abuser will blame you. Although it is probably your nature to try to get along with others and not make unnecessary waves, you must learn to stop trying to please your abuser because it is an impossible task. Therefore, set boundaries and stick to them when verbally and emotionally abused.

It is important to do the following:

- Confront the problem.
- Verbalize what is in your heart and on your mind, instead of internalizing your feelings. Speak it out!
- Let others know that you have been wounded by the abusive behavior and that you will no longer tolerate the abuse and announce the consequences.

Strategies

- Enforce the consequence each time the abuser violates the request.
- Take responsibility for yourself and refuse to be defensive, retreat into a shell, or play the "victim" role.

The mind of a discerning person gains knowledge, while the ears of wise people seek out knowledge.
                                         Proverbs 18:15, ISV

The book of Proverbs provided me much wisdom in dealing with difficult people. Proverbs 22:24, for example, reminds us not to make friends with a hot-tempered person and not to associate with people who are easily angered.

Strategy # 6: Understand that No One Can Make You a Victim without Your Consent

If God is for [you], who can be against [you]?
                                                Romans 8:31

To be treated with respect is God's will for you. It is also His will that you remove yourself from an abusive situation.

> *Honor all people. Love the brotherhood. Fear God. Honor the king.*
> 1 Peter 2:17, NKJV

> *Not giving up meeting together, as some are in the habit of doing, but encouraging one another—and all the more as you see the Day approaching.*
> Hebrews 10:25

Strategy # 7: Rediscover Your True Self; Do Things that Bring You Peace, Joy, and Pleasure

Recognize that you are never alone. The Lord has promised never to leave you nor forsake you. He will never let you down, unlike the abusers in your life.

Realize that everyone experiences pain and brokenness; it's a part of life. Ask the Lord to heal the pain of your past and soothe your soul as you take refuge in Him and draw on His strength (see Psalm 18:2).

Make a self-analysis of your likes and dislikes. As with most oppressed people, you may be an individual who has a sincere desire to please others, but therein could be a trap for you. It is okay for you to make those observations. You do not have to deny your likes and dislikes.

Strategies

 We victims often focus on the needs of others while ignoring our own well-being. That behavior is neither safe nor healthy.

 Remind yourself that life is short and that God did not create you to be a doormat for others. Discover how to live life like God is your first response rather than your last resort.

The Victor's Prayer

Heavenly Father,
I lack wisdom
and spiritual understanding.
So, I ask that You generously
give me the wisdom and vigilance
to stay clear of those
who do not have
my best interests at heart.
Lord, keep me close to You
each and every day.
Thank You for answering my prayer.
In the name of Jesus, I pray,
Amen!

Be Vigilant (Not Gaslighted!)

Ye shall know the truth, and the truth shall make you free. John 8:32, KJV

As the Lord was with Joseph
(Genesis Chapters 37-50),
so has the Lord been with Jan!

Power Key #6

Be Forgiving

For if you forgive other people when they sin against you, your heavenly Father will also forgive you. But if you do not forgive others their sins, your heavenly Father will not forgive your sins.   Matthew 6:14-15

To move from victim to victory and recover from the trauma and drama of domestic abuse, one has to learn how to be forgiving.

The Complexity of Forgiveness

They are three simple, yet complex words: "I forgive you." Ordinarily, those three words are not difficult to say or understand, but forgiveness had become a big problem for me. Even though I knew it was the right thing to do, forgiving my two former husbands (who hurt me deeply) was tough. And I suspect that I'm not alone in my struggle with forgiveness.

What Is Forgiveness?

Forgiveness means "to let go," as when a person does not demand payment for a debt. We forgive others when we let go of resentment and give up any claim to be compensated for the hurt or loss we have suffered. The Bible teaches that unselfish love is the basis for true forgiveness, since love *"does not remember wrongs done against it"* (1 Corinthians 13:4-5, ICB).

Forgiveness is:
- Commanded by Almighty God
- Extending grace to the person responsible for the offense
- A gift to the one who least deserves it
- Something you must do as much for yourself as for the other person
- Impossible without God's help
- Waiving penalty or punishment
- Evidence of spiritual growth
- Heart lifting
- Freedom to let go of something you would rather hold on to
- An inside job
- Supernatural empowerment by God
- Being spiritually healthy and Christ-like
- Releasing or freeing the one who has hurt you
- Extending mercy

From Victim to Victory

Once I studied the definition of forgiveness, I realized that I had a problem with it. Both former husbands had hurt me deeply, but differently. Vincent (Husband Number One) was unsaved, unstable, physically violent, bipolar, and suffering from obsessive compulsive disorder (OCD).[1] He hated "religious people" and called them all hypocrites–including me.

On the other hand, Harry (Husband Number Two) gave the appearance of stability and professed his faith in God. He was a charismatic minister of the Gospel and could preach and teach the Word of God with authority, clarity, simplicity, and passion. He could do it all, but, in actuality, he was a phony, a crook, and an imposter.[2]

Even years after the separation and divorce from both husbands, I still continued to hold a grudge and felt anger and resentment against one or both of these men. I had said to myself and others that I forgave them, but, in all honesty, I hadn't.

Two Reasons for My Reluctance to Forgive

Let us not kid ourselves. Forgiveness is neither natural nor comfortable. Forgiving those who have done us wrong does not come quickly or easily. This should not have been a surprise to me, but, for some reason, it was.

---

1. See *Testimony of a Kept Woman*, pp. 61 - 65)
2. See *Testimony of a Kept Woman*, pp. 193-196

Be Forgiving

There were at least two reasons I didn't want to forgive my two exes.

#1. I Felt that My Exes Did Not Deserve My Forgiveness: When I thought about all those two rascals had done to me, I didn't want to forgive them because they didn't deserve my forgiveness. I wanted to hold them hostage, take revenge, and make them pay. I believed *they* should have been asking *me* to forgive *them*.

Honestly speaking, I thought I deserved a badge of honor for not landing in the state penitentiary for premeditated murder. I was a saint compared to them.

But it was hard for me to act righteous and holy when all I wanted to think about was how I could get even with the two men who had caused me so much pain. It was hard to take the high road when my mind was preoccupied with how I would react when they both came crawling back to me, begging and pleading for my forgiveness, and desperate for me to take them back. Yes, it was hard to forgive when my thoughts were preoccupied with revenge.

#2. I Somehow Felt that Forgiveness Was a Sign of Weakness: Most victims of domestic abuse are considered to be weak, enablers of their abusers, and wishy-washy. Being weak was the last thing I wanted to be thought of. But, when it boils right down to it, forgiveness is not weakness. There is absolutely nothing harder to do than to forgive a person for the wrongs they have committed against you, especially when the pain was planned and orchestrated to cut to the very core of your being.

Someone might ask the question, "Aren't you a Christian?" And I would reply, "Yes, I am a Christian. And yes, I clearly understand that forgiveness is a fundamental concept of my faith. And yes, I also know that if I want God to forgive me of my transgressions against others, then I must also forgive those who have transgressed against me." However, somehow knowing all this did not make forgiving my two former husbands any easier.

I Finally Realized that Forgiveness Is Not:
- Letting the offending person off the hook without consequences
- Making excuses for the other person's behavior
- Saying that the offense does not matter (dismissing it)
- Forgetting hurt feelings
- Circumventing divine retribution or the reaping of consequences
- Being a doormat
- Forgetting the past

- Natural or spontaneous
- Reconciliation
- Earned
- Conditional
- Impossible

I Considered the High Cost of Unforgiveness:

There were times when I didn't feel like reading my Bible and memorizing scriptures that were certain to keep me in the right frame of mind. There were even times when I wanted to get "down and dirty." I didn't want to do the right thing. I didn't want to be good because I felt that revenge would make me feel so much better. That was my carnal nature talking. But, in my spirit, I understood that I had to forgive because it was better for me.

Unforgiveness:

- Robs you of God's forgiveness (see Mark 11:35).
- Grieves the Holy Spirit (see Ephesians 4:30-32).
- Grows roots of bitterness (see Hebrews 12:15).
- Keeps you a prisoner of sin (see Acts 8:23).

I had to find the strength to forgive. I didn't want to grow old, ugly, and filled with bitterness and anger. No, life was too short for that nonsense. So, I started my Google search of the Scriptures on "forgiveness." I was amazed at the number of verses displayed.

From Victim to Victory

GOD'S WORD SAYS A LOT ABOUT FORGIVENESS

Be kind and compassionate to one another, forgiving each other, just as in Christ God forgave you. Ephesians 4:32

Then Peter came to Jesus and asked, "Lord, how many times shall I forgive my brother or sister who sins against me? Up to seven times?" Jesus answered, "I tell you, not seven times, but seventy-seven times." Matthew 18: 21-22

Therefore, as God's chosen people, holy and dearly loved, clothe yourselves with compassion, kindness, humility, gentleness and patience. Bear with each other and forgive one another if any of you has a grievance against someone. Forgive as the Lord forgave you. Colossians 3:12-13

Never pay back evil for evil to anyone. Respect what is right in the sight of all men.
Romans 12:17, NASB

Whoever would foster love covers over an offense, but whoever repeats the matter separates close friends.
Proverbs 17:9

Be Forgiving

If we confess our sins, he is faithful and just to forgive us our sins, and to cleanse us from all unrighteousness. 1 John 1:9, KJV

The more I studied the Scriptures, the more I could feel my cold, hard, broken heart softening. But I knew my journey was far from over. The anger in me still boiled up from time to time, when I thought about the harsh treatment I had endured. I had to continue my study. Ending too soon was sure to result in my becoming an "angry black woman," which is bad enough, but I would be in jeopardy also of becoming an "old angry black woman," and I didn't want any part of that!

Yes, I had done everything I could to make both marriages work. Yes, I had done more than my fair share. But I had to stop keeping score and pray that God would help me to forgive both men and cleanse my heart so that I could be a useful vessel for Him.

But What About Self-Forgiveness?

In looking back over the list of what forgiveness is, I realized that my real problem was not so much about me not forgiving my two former husbands as it was that I had not forgiven myself. Why had I not forgiven me? It's complicated, but unconsciously I had been holding on to

From Victim to Victory

something that had happened many years before when I was in my sophomore year in college. Somehow, I felt that I didn't deserve happiness, fulfillment, and peace because of what I had done. I had forfeited my right to be forgiven.

Because I grew up in a legalistic, religious church that taught that some sins were beyond redemption, and there was an unpardonable sin, I was traumatized. I didn't tell anyone about what had happened that night while on a date with Vincent when I lost my virginity in the back seat of his car.[3] I was too ashamed to tell anyone, even my mother. So, I continued to hold on to the erroneous belief that I had committed the unpardonable sin. For years, I kept that emotional crisis in my life a secret and tried to deal with the consequences of my unforgivable sin by myself.

Vincent took advantage of my trauma and used my grief as a weapon of power and control, to gain the upper hand in our marital relationship. His violence was used to keep me in line and to punish me for committing the sin to pass all sins. My misconception about the unpardonable sin, my error in my the interpretation of the Scriptures had kept me bound in strongholds since I was nineteen. My low self-esteem—from guilt, embarrassment, and shame—had restricted me and held me in bondage all that time. I stayed in a physically violent

3. See *Testimony of a Kept Woman* pp. 42-43

Be Forgiving

marriage because I felt that I deserved to be punished, and I was merely reaping what I had sown.

Even after I knew the truth that my heavenly Father loved me and sent His only begotten Son, Jesus Christ, to earth to die for me, I still couldn't break free on my own. I needed the supernatural empowerment of God to release me from my guilt and enable me to forgive myself and finally be free.

With a new-found revelation, the Holy Spirit led me to read from Isaiah 53:

> *Who believes what we've heard and seen?*
>   *Who would have thought God's saving power*
>   *would look like this?*
>
> *The servant grew up before God—a scrawny seedling,*
>   *a scrubby plant in a parched field.*
> *There was nothing attractive about him,*
>   *nothing to cause us to take a second look.*
> *He was looked down on and passed over,*
>   *a man who suffered, who knew pain firsthand.*
> *One look at him and people turned away.*
>   *We looked down on him, thought he was scum.*
> *But the fact is, it was our pains he carried—*
>   *our disfigurements, all the things wrong with us.*

From Victim to Victory

We thought he brought it on himself,
 that God was punishing him for his failures.
But it was our sins that did that to him,
 that ripped and tore and crushed him—our sins!
He took the punishment, and that made us whole.
Through his bruises, we get healed.
We're all like sheep who've wandered off and gotten lost.
 We've all done our own thing, gone our way.
And God has piled all our sins, everything we've done wrong,
 on him, on him.

He was beaten; he was tortured,
 but he didn't say a word.
Like a lamb taken to be slaughtered
 and like a sheep being sheared,
 he took it all in silence.
Justice miscarried, and he was led off—
 and did anyone really know what was happening?
He died without a thought for his own welfare,
 beaten bloody for the sins of my people.
They buried him with the wicked,
 threw him in a grave with a rich man,
Even though he'd never hurt a soul
 or said one word that wasn't true.

Still, it's what God had in mind all along,
  to crush him with pain.
The plan was that he give himself as an offering for sin
  so that he'd see life come from it—life, life, and more life.
  And God's plan will deeply prosper through him.

Out of that terrible travail of soul,
  he'll see that it's worth it and be glad he did it.
Through what he experienced, my righteous one,
    my servant,
  will make many "righteous ones,"
  as he himself carries the burden of their sins.
Therefore I'll reward him extravagantly—
  the best of everything, the highest honors—
Because he looked death in the face and didn't flinch
  because he embraced the company of the lowest.
He took on his shoulders the sin of the many;
  he took up the cause of all the black sheep.
                              Isaiah 53:1-12, MSG

EMPOWERED BY SELF-FORGIVENESS.

After reading Isaiah 53 and seeing what my Lord Jesus had done for me, a light came on in my head. I was ready to forgive both husbands and myself. God the Father had given me the keys to unlock my self-imposed prison and walk out a free woman and to live my life to the fullest.

What Jesus did changed my life:

> *For God so loved the world that he gave his one and only Son, that whoever believes in him shall not perish but have eternal life. For God didn't send his Son into the world to judge the world, but that the world should be saved through him.* John 3:16-17, WEB

Just knowing that God loved me so much that He would send His only begotten Son Jesus down here to die for me was amazing. But to think that Jesus, the Son of God, loved me so much that He was willing to leave the glories of Heaven and come down and live in this dark and sinful world just to die for me ... well, that was mind boggling and mind transforming. Suddenly Romans 12:2 came alive for me:

> *Do not conform to the pattern of this world, but be transformed by the renewing of your mind.*

My mind was changed. I had been living a lie. God was not angry with me because I had fallen short of His glory. He knew I wouldn't be able to do everything right—even from the beginning. And that is why God the Father, God the Son, and God the Holy Spirit formed a divine plan of redemption before the foundation of the world. I had believed a lie, that I had committed the unpardonable sin and was too far gone for Christ to forgive me. That was nonsense. I had been duped by a lie, but no more. Jesus said:

You will know the truth, and the truth will set you free.
John 8:32

My two former husbands were free. I had loosed them and let them both go in my mind, in my heart, and in my spirit. But, more importantly, I had forgiven myself. I now knew that forgiveness was greater than vengeance, and compassion greater than anger.

Praise be to God! I have been forgiven. All my sins are forgiven and forgotten because of the righteousness of Jesus Christ on my behalf, and yours are forgiven too!

TO GOD BE THE GLORY!

―― An Important Question ――

So, how will you move from victim to victory and be forgiving?

Strategies

Strategy # 1: Recognize Your Need to Forgive

The Lord enabled me to admit my sins to Him and restore my relationship. With opened eyes, the scales of stubbornness fell off, and I was able to see clearly.

> *If we are faithless,*
> *he remains faithful,*
> *for he cannot disown himself.* 2 Timothy 2:13

> *If we confess our sins, he is faithful and just and will forgive us our sins and purify us from all unrighteousness.* 1 John 1:9

Strategy # 2: Choose to Forgive Others

Our feelings do not dictate our forgiveness. I would never have forgiven if I had waited until I "felt" like it. Instead, I chose to obey God and steadfastly resist the devil in his attempts to poison me with bitter thoughts. I made a quality decision to forgive, and, as a result, God healed my wounded emotions in time (see Matthew 6:12-14).

Strategy # 3: Accept The Fact That You Are Powerless To Forgive Without the Help of the Holy Spirit

It was impossible for me to do it on my own. I had to humble myself and cry out to God for His help. In John 20:22, Jesus breathed on the disciples and said, *"Receive the Holy Spirit!"* His very next instruction was about forgiveness. The presence of His Spirit in your life will enable you to forgive.

Strategy # 4: Recognize You Need to Forgive Yourself

Realize that you must forgive those who have sinned against you, but don't forget to forgive yourself. God loves you, and He has sent His Son Jesus to die for your sins. He said, *"IT IS FINISHED!"* (John 19:30).

Strategy # 5: View Your Abusers from a Different Perspective

The Holy Spirit can give you a new way of looking at others. Begin to see your abusers, not as they have been to you, but rather as the people they might become if they desired the indwelling of the Holy Spirit. We are all a work in progress.

The results of forgiving those who have hurt you deeply will be to find joy in your journey, wholeness for your wounds and hurts, and praise for your pain. God can remove your anger and restore your sense of peace. When you learn to think about good things and forgive others, He will make you BRAND NEW!

Blessed is he whose transgression is forgiven,
Whose sin is covered.
Blessed is the man to whom the LORD does not impute iniquity,
And in whose spirit, there is no deceit.
          Psalm 32:1-2, NKJV

As you move from victim to victor, you will realize that forgiveness is greater than vengeance, and compassion greater than anger. My personal philosophy has become: I cannot hate my two former husbands for mistreating me; I must, rather, pity the both of them because they, too, were victims in their own way. Because the world and their own fathers abandoned them, they had a negative ideal of masculinity thrust on them (which I refuse to subscribe to for my sons and grandson).

> *For You, Lord, are good, and ready to forgive,*
> *And abundant in lovingkindness to all who call upon You.*   Psalm 86:5, NKJV

Again, discover how to live life like *God* is your *first response* rather than your *last resort*.

The Victor's Prayer

Dear Heavenly Father,
I choose, as an act of my will, regardless of my feelings,
to forgive the persons
who have wronged me.
I release them
and set myself free
to receive Your healing.
With Your help,
I will no longer dwell on the situations
or continue to talk about them.
I thank You for forgiving me,
as I have forgiven them all.
I ask this in Jesus' name,
Amen!

From Victim to Victory

> *Ye shall know the truth, and the truth shall make you free.* — John 8:32, KJV

As the Lord was with Joseph
(Genesis Chapters 37-50),
so has the Lord been with Jan!

Power Key #7

BE VICTORIOUS!
(YOU ARE A WINNER)

But thanks be to God, who gives us the victory through our Lord Jesus Christ.
1 Corinthians 15:57, NKJV

"For I know the plans I have for you," declares the LORD, "plans to prosper you and not to harm you, plans to give you hope and a future."   Jeremiah 29:11

LIVING THROUGH TEARS, TRIALS, AND TROUBLE IS TERRIBLE, YET WONDERFUL

   I was helpless and hopeless without Jesus Christ. I tried to do things my own way, but the end results were always the same: TOTAL FAILURE. As I continued to think and act like a victim of domestic abuse, I continued in a Catch-22 downward spiral.

What I needed to happen in my life was a paradigm shift. I required an entirely different mindset. I needed a reset button for the computer of my mind.

IRONICALLY, ABUSE BECAME MY PROGRESS

> *And we know that God causes all things to work together for good for those who love God, who are called according to his purpose for them. For God knew his people in advance, and he chose them to become like his Son, so that his Son would be the firstborn among many brothers and sisters.*
>
> Romans 8:28-29, NLT

God is amazing! Just imagine, if I had been blessed with a happy marriage and lived with my spouse and celebrated our 50th Wedding Anniversary, like my parents and my aunts and uncles:

- I would not be writing books about domestic violence and emotional and verbal abuse.

- I would not have been called into the ministry to preach the Word of God.

- I would not have been blessed to teach and witness

to those who are in pain—embarrassed, hurting, and bewildered.

- I would never have understood the plight and predicament of millions trapped and bound in domestic abuse—physical, psychological, emotional, verbal and sexual

How could I have given my testimony and witness to millions of abused and hurting people of all ages and walks of life? How could there have been *"A Kept Woman"* who went from *"Misery to Ministry Instead of the State Penitentiary?"* How could I have endured forty-two years of abuse:

- Almost two decades with Husband Number One, who was violent and bipolar and suffered from OCD

- Twenty-two years with Husband Number Two, who was a smooth-walking, sweet-talking, sociopath (it was always about him).

How could I have survived and become victorious, to overcome and walk in God's plan, purpose, and destiny for my life?

It took God's divine destiny for me to be called, used, and molded, to enable me to become a mentor and model for victims.

- God uses a "mess" to write His message.
- God uses tests to fashion His testimony.
- God uses trouble to produce His triumph.
- God uses victimization to form his victorious endings.
- God is using my story to bring Him glory, and He will use your story, too.

And we know that in all things God works for the good of those who love him, who have been called according to his purpose. Romans 8:28

I was designed and destined to do this. It was my divine destiny. There are no "accidents" in this journey called life, just divine appointments. No experiences are wasted by God. He recycles the good, the bad, and the ugly, to reproduce the impossible.

Domestic violence is universal and pervasive, and it transcends race, color, and economic and social ramifications. Only God can transform this grotesque ugliness into His gracious and unimaginable uniqueness for His glory.

God wants you to remember that your present situation is not your final destination. Success is not what you have, but Who you have. His name is Jesus.

Be Victorious!

THERE WAS TREASURE IN MY TRIAL

I had been a victim of both physical domestic violence and emotional and verbal abuse, and I needed wisdom to navigate between the opposing forces of abuse to create a new life for myself. For nearly forty-two years I lived under threats, bullying, terror, and intimidation. There was a time when I was a broken, weak, and silent victim. I was a woman who had low self-esteem and low self-worth.

It takes great courage to be obedient to God and begin to live counter-culture. You look foolish and neurotic to others when you live according to your faith in God, but in the end, you are victorious. So, live life like God is your first response, rather than your last resort.

Yes, I am a survivor and an overcomer of physical, verbal, and emotional domestic abuse, but I must daily pray for God's protection and deliverance from the lies and deception of those who would want to deceive me and place me back into strongholds and bondage. We all face a real battle between good and evil every day, but Jesus died so that we can have victory—now and forever.

Jesus is faithful and true, and we can trust Him to do everything He has promised to do for us in His Word. We can rest assured with the peace and confidence of God.

From Victim to Victory

> *Thanks be to God who gives us the victory through our Lord Jesus Christ.*   1 Corinthians 15:57, NKJV

There Was Divine Destiny in My Darkness

I give all praise, honor, and glory to my Lord and Savior Jesus Christ. It was His grace and mercy that changed me. He enabled me to no longer continue to conform to the world of domestic abuse. Instead, He transformed me by the renewing of my mind. In other words, I used to see my desperate plight and situation with my limited eyesight. I struggled with fear and brokenness … until I learned to view my domestic abuse as a stronghold that could be broken with a new vision from my heart. Therefore, without vision, there could never have been any change in my desperate situation.

There is an Old Testament scripture that has literally changed my life and enabled me to think differently. It was written by the wisest man who has ever lived. His name was King Solomon, and he was the son of King David. Solomon wrote more than three thousand proverbs. Here is a sampling:

> *Where there is no vision, the people are unrestrained.*
>   Proverbs 29:18, NASB

Another Old Testament scripture that compliments Solomon's proverb and gives me spiritual strength is this:

Be Victorious!

My people are destroyed for lack of knowledge.
                                        Hosea 4:6, NASB

Previously, I had little or no spiritual vision. My life went from one crisis to another. Life was so dreadful that I didn't want to leave work and go home. I hated the weekends because I was unable to hide out at my workplace. I had to be in my house, a place where the atmosphere was filled with gloom, doom, dysfunction, and abuse. I would rather have been at work because that's where I experienced peace and acceptance. It is sad, but true, that I felt more relaxed and calm at work than I ever did in my own home.

Conversely, everyone else at work looked forward to the weekends. They were more excited and upbeat as the week drew closer to Friday. But not me. I looked to the weekends with dread and fear, because Husband Number One was at his worst on the weekends. It was at home where he would have his mood changes. It was at home on the weekends when he would become upset, angry, and violent for seemingly no reason at all. On weekends, my boys and I walked around the house as if on eggshells.

However, there came a time when something had to give. Enough was enough. It took a crisis to help me change my way of thinking and begin to apply what I was learning from God's

Word. No longer would I maintain the *status quo*. Things were becoming intolerable at home. No longer would I continue to see myself as a helpless victim. What I was doing was not working, and something had to change. The change was about to happen, and it would happen first in my head.

Four Steps in My Struggle for Victory

1. I Had to Reason Within: The moment I decided to make a change in my situation, there was an inner struggle going on within. The question, as always, was: "Should I stay or should I go?" I would begin to argue with myself. There was a debate going on in my mind. There seemed to be two different conversations going on in my head at once. One voice was telling me that it was my own fault, that I was responsible for the mess I was in, while the other voice said that it didn't matter. Everything was going to be all right. These voices argued in my head:

- The voice of TRUTH and the voice of ERROR
- The voice of RESPONSIBILITY and the voice of EXCUSES
- The voice of FAITH and the voice of FEAR
- The voice of CHANGE and the voice of STUBBORNNESS

Be Victorious!

I heard additional voices with questions in my head. One voice would say, "It's not so bad. My husband will change." But the other voice would answer, "But, you are already in a desperate hole, and those excuses will not get you out of there."

- Should I stay or should I go?
- What if I leave and I need to come back?
- What if I jump out of the proverbial frying pan into the fire?
- What if I fail again and get rejected?
- How would I survive the increased pain?
- What if I walked out and couldn't make it on my own?
- What if things didn't work out for me on my own?
- What if I failed and people laughed at me? I would look like a fool—as if I didn't already look like one.

Both voices continued in my mind. The question was, "Which voice would I listen to and heed?"

2. I Had to Take Personal Responsibility for My Mistakes: After I went through all the mental gymnastics and thought it all through, I had to make a personal decision, a resolution. After much prayer and meditation, I knew what I had to do. The voice of wisdom and reason had won the argument. It was time to do for myself what no one else could do for me.

I decided to take personal ownership of my choice. No one could live my life for me. It was not about others. It was about *me*. It was *my* life, and when I decided to get up and move on, I had to realize that there would be people who would talk about me.

Yes, I would be the topic of the gossip mills. Yes, there would be a few who would laugh at me, but regardless of what others would think or say, I knew what I must do.

3. I Had to Resolve to Make the Necessary Changes: I decided to rise up and move forward. I knew I had to make a change. No matter how long I had stayed in my pit of despair, it was better for me to rise up and make a U-turn now. No longer could I continue to remain on this path of destruction that would surely lead straight to further heartache and, eventually, tragedy.

Although it was not easy, I had come to the realization that I had made a mistake, and I had a choice to make.

4. I Had to Begin a U-Turn: I made a choice, to make a U-turn back to God spiritually. It was a U-turn in my attitude. I had to be willing to say that I had made a mistake and I needed to change. Making U-turns can be fearful. It can be intimidating. But it is better to move on to the right path than continuing to stroll down the wrong road.

Be Victorious!

Jesus told the story of the Prodigal Son. That son showed us how to make a U-turn (see Luke 15:11–32*).* No matter how far or how long I had been on the wrong road, I realized that there was a better way. And I am so glad that God made that way a for me.

There Is Nothing More Powerful Than a Changed Mind

My life was nearly destroyed. However, today it is entirely different. I have learned to think of every day as the first day of the beginning of my life. I have gained knowledge, wisdom, and strategies to help me learn and recover from the abuse I endured. Through Christ, I have learned that we all make mistakes and take miss-steps. Each one of us has missed the mark of perfection in one way or another. There is nothing to be ashamed of, unless we continue to stay and wallow in the muck and mire of life.

Going from Victim to Victory

If this is where you are, and you feel you need to make a U-turn in your life, take the time to go through these four steps:

1. Reason within yourself.
2. Take personal responsibility for your mistakes.
3. Resolve to make the necessary changes.
4. Begin your u-turn.

From Victim to Victory

I learned (the hard way) that I did not have to stay the way I was. Anytime I was ready. I could have said to myself, "Enough is enough!" It was a matter of changing my thoughts and refocusing my vision. Today I can move forward through Christ Jesus.

Remember: the journey of a thousand miles begins with the first step. God wants you to remember that your present situation is not your final destination.

To God be the Glory!

—— An Important Question ——

So, how will you recover from the trauma and drama of emotional domestic violence and move from victim to victory?

Strategies

As a reminder: These are the strategies God used with me, but the strategies He used with me may not necessarily be the same strategies He will use with you. God is awesome, and His strategies and solutions are not the "cookie-cutter" variety. He is not confined to one-size-fits-all solutions, and He will not be placed in a box. The problems of domestic abuse are similar, but escape plans can vary significantly. Although no two situations are exactly the same, God will give you the solutions to your own unique problems. Look at my strategies and then craft your own exit plan. God is creative, powerful, awesome, and absolutely faithful. The rest is up to you.

Strategy # 1: Learn from Your Past Experiences

Milk every lesson the Lord God is teaching you, so that you never repeat your shame and pain. You can either:

- Dwell on your brokenness
- Cover up your brokenness

- Ignore your brokenness
- Deal with your brokenness and find life-changing lessons in it.

Strategy # 2: Make Time to Read God's Word, Pray, and Be Alone with Him

If you desire to be closer to the Lord God and strengthen your existing shallow relationship, then make time to pray, and make time to be alone with Him. Intimacy with God is not automatic, and it does not happen by coincidence. It happens on purpose.

All kinds of abuse—physical violence, emotional and verbal abuse, etc.—originate from a spirit. Dealing with it requires spiritual warfare, so you must prepare yourself to fight.

Put on the full armor of God, so that you can take your stand against the devil's schemes.
         Ephesians 6:11, NASB

You will seek Me and find Me when you search for Me with all your heart. Jeremiah 29:13, NASB

Your secrets for success will come from time spent in solitude with the Great Shepherd.

Strategy # 3: Realize that There Is Purpose in Your Pain

The fact that God allowed you to go through pain lets you know there is a reason for it. If you allow Him to, God will use your pain and victimization to bring glory and praise to Him and good for you.

You have a choice. Change how you think. Remember, you have choices to transform yourself from victimization to victory. You don't have to remain a victim. You can choose your thoughts and actions. God has given you the ability and power to go in another direction. Make the Lord Jesus glad and the devil mad. Tell your story. Give your testimony.

Strategy # 4: Think on What Is True, Not Alternative Facts

Change your perception of who you are, and you change who you are. It's all in the mind. Nothing is stronger than a changed mind.

> *Finally, brothers and sisters, whatever is true, whatever is noble, whatever is right, whatever is pure, whatever is lovely, whatever is admirable—if any-*

thing is excellent or praiseworthy—think about such things.   Philippians 4:8

It's true. You are not what you think you are, but what you think, you are.

Obtain a mind-shift. Develop a new mental pattern for thinking. Retrain your mind to seek the truth. Concentrate and think on things that are noble, just, right, dignified, and spiritually mature. Guard your mind and retrain your thoughts to think with the mind of Christ.

Stop thinking about things that would cause you to produce anger, bitterness, or resentment. Develop a discipline of rejection. Jesus said:

And you will know the truth, and the truth will make you free.   John 8:32, NASB

Read and believe Ephesians 3:20:

Now unto him, that is able to do exceeding abundantly above all that we ask or think, according to the power that worketh in us.   Ephesians 3:20, KJV

Strategy # 5: Release Your Past and Reach Forward to Your Future

You can't change your past, but you *can* do something different with your future. Realize that it's up to you.

The apostle Paul wrote:

I do not consider myself yet to have taken hold of it. But one thing I do: Forgetting what is behind and straining toward what is ahead, I press on toward the goal to win the prize for which God has called me heavenward in Christ Jesus. Philippians 3:13-14

Forget the past and press forward to what God has ahead for you.

Forget the former things;
  do not dwell on the past.
See, I am doing a new thing!
  Now it springs up; do you not perceive it?
I am making a way in the wilderness
  and streams in the wasteland. Isaiah 43:18-19

Therefore if any man be in Christ, he is a new creature: old things are passed away; behold, all things are become new. 2 Corinthians 5:17, KJV

Strategies

But they that wait upon the LORD shall renew their strength; they shall mount up with wings as eagles; they shall run, and not be weary; and they shall walk, and not faint.   Isaiah 40:31, KJV

The Holy Spirit will re-program your mind, and you will be transformed, from the inside out.

Don't become so well-adjusted to your culture that you fit into it without even thinking. Instead, fix your attention on God. You'll be changed from the inside out. Readily recognize what he wants from you, and quickly respond to it. Unlike the culture around you, always dragging you down to its level of immaturity, God brings the best out of you, develops well-formed maturity in you.
                                              Romans 12:2, MSG

Only the Lord Jesus Christ turned Jan's negative experience with domestic violence and emotional and verbal abuse into a positive. To God be the Glory! Instead of Jan's life becoming something of despair, to the point of overwhelming her, God used those negative circumstances and that unfamiliar place to continue her relationship with Jesus and the Holy Spirit.

Strategy # 6: Decide Not to Stay in Domestic Abuse One Minute Longer than Necessary (see Romans 12:2)

It is not the Lord's will for you to live in chaos and fear.

For the Spirit God gave us does not make us timid, but it gives us power, love, and self-discipline.
                                        2 Timothy 1:7

Slowly, but surely, the Lord will transform you into a courageous person of faith. His presence will be impressive. He will empower you to overcome your low self-esteem. But do not remain in a violent situation any longer than necessary, and do not allow guilt and condemnation to keep you in mental chains. There is no condemnation in Christ Jesus (see Romans 8:1).

All you need to do is confess your sin and move on. Jesus has already paid the price for you. Don't continue "beating yourself up" for what you did years ago. Learn to hear God's voice, and go when He says, "Go!"

Strategy # 7: Visualize Your Future Success and Move Forward with Intentionality!

Keep repeating to yourself:

I can do all things through him who gives me strength.   Philippians 4:13

Realize that you are not powerless, and take the authority to choose your thoughts. Understand that is important for you to choose carefully. Read and memorize this verse, and then say it often. There is power in God's promises.

> *Finally, believers, whatever is true, whatever is honorable and worthy of respect, whatever is right and confirmed by God's word, whatever is pure and wholesome, whatever is lovely and brings peace, whatever is admirable and of good repute; if there is any excellence, if there is anything worthy of praise think continually on these things [center your mind on them, and implant them in your heart].*   Philippians 4:8, AMP

Jesus said that He had come for me to have life and have it abundantly (see John 10:10), and yet I had allowed the thief to steal, kill, and destroy my life—all because I was thinking and acting out of fear. Now I realize that God's Son came to give me life abundantly. You can trust Him with everything in your life: your circumstances, your difficulties, your needs, and your doubts.

STRATEGY # 8: NO ONE CAN MAKE YOU A VICTIM WITHOUT YOUR CONSENT

Never give up! Your past does not define your destiny! Discover how to live life like God is your first response and not your last resort.

If God is for [you], who can be against [you]?
Romans 8:31

The answer to that question is clear: absolutely nobody!

Therefore, my beloved brethren, be ye steadfast, unmovable, always abounding in the work of the Lord, forasmuch as ye know that your labor is not in vain in the Lord. 1 Corinthians 15:58, KJV

Strategies

And we know that all things work together for good to them that love God, to them who are the called according to his purpose. Romans 8:28, KJV

Remember, your present situation is not your final destination.

BE VICTORIOUS!
YOU ARE A WINNER,
AND NO ONE CAN STOP YOU!

THE VICTOR'S PRAYER

Dear Heavenly Father,
Thank You for Your Word.
Thank You for giving me
Your divine wisdom.
Lord, thank You
for giving me the victory
through Your beloved Son,
Jesus Christ.
Yours in Christ Jesus,
Amen!

Be Victorious!

Ye shall know the truth, and the truth shall make you free. John 8:32, KJV

No matter who you are or what you have done, "God Loves You with a perfect (*agape*) love (see 1 John 4:8).

As the Lord was with Joseph
(Genesis chapters 37-50),
so has the Lord been with Jan
and with You!

Questions for Reflection and Group Discussion

1. What does it mean to be victorious? _____
_____
_____
_____

2. If victims have choices, why are they victimized? _____
_____
_____
_____

3. Why did I say that living through tears, trials, and troubles was terrible, yet wonderful? _____
_____
_____
_____

4. How did abuse ironically become my progress? _____

Questions for Reflection and Group Discussion

_____
_____
_____

5. Explain how there was treasure in my trial? _____
_____
_____
_____

6. What did I say were the four steps to my victory over domestic abuse?
   1) _____
   2) _____
   3) _____
   4) _____

7. Why is having a changed mind vitally important for a victim of domestic abuse? _____
_____
_____
_____

8. Out of the seven principles suggested for recovery, which one will you try to implement first? Explain. _____
_____
_____

_____
_____

9. In what way did you find this Guide helpful? Please explain. _____
_____
_____
_____

10. What other areas of domestic abuse would you have liked for me to address? Explain. _____
_____
_____
_____

Please Note: If there are additional areas of concern that you would like Jan to address, please contact her by email at ***jan-newellbyrd@gmail.com***

Epilogue

(Vincent's Conversion and Transformation: No One Could Have Ever Imagined)

A Bad Beginning

From the start, Vincent and I were total opposites. Even though we had few things in common, we got married during our third year as undergraduates in college. It is true that opposites attract, but it's equally true that they later repel. For one thing, I loved people, but Vincent didn't like people at all. I had a close relationship with my family, especially my mother and his. His mother even called me her "daughter-in-love." But Vincent had a strained relationship with his mom. They never got along well.

Finally, Enough Was Enough!

Vincent and I graduated from college together in 1961 and worked as classroom teachers in the Gary, Indiana Community School System. We later returned to graduate school and earned our master's degree in administration and supervision. We were blessed to became the first husband and wife elementary school principal team in the early 1970s.

Observing us from the outside in, we looked like the ideal up-and-coming couple. But even with our successful professional careers, our marriage was in serious trouble. Vincent was mentally brilliant, but his lack of anger management skills and anti-social behavior made him miserable at work. When he returned home in the evenings, he would take out his frustrations on me and our sons.

As Vincent slipped deeper into dark moods of aggression and anger, he became increasingly irritated and hostile and physically violent. Our two boys, Dexter and Lawrence, were becoming painfully aware of the dysfunction in our family. There were times when Vincent would explode into anger and blame and attack me for everything that went wrong in his life. Our sons would try to intervene and separate the two of us, to protect me, their mother.

I could see the proverbial "handwriting on the wall." It was inevitable that sooner or later tragedy would erupt—if drastic measures were not taken. I didn't want a divorce because I did not want my children coming from a broken home, but it was transparently clear that I had to do something different! Something had to change.

Epilogue

One day my sons confided to me, in desperation and frustration, "We don't have a home! All we have is a house, and it's already broken, Mom!" Those words from my two children not only caught my attention; they almost broke my heart. What had I done? Why had I forced two innocent souls to endure domestic violence and abuse, just because I wanted to live in a fantasy world of normalcy? How terrible! I needed to make an immediate decision.

Finally, enough was enough! At that moment, the scales of self-deception fell from my eyes, and I found the courage, strength, and good sense to do what I should have done a long time before. I made secret plans, and I prepared to leave Vincent and take the children with me.[1]

My Continued Close Relationship with Former In-Laws

Vincent and I separated in 1976 and later divorced, but Vincent's mother and I continued to have a close relationship. She knew about her son's problems, but we never once discussed them. It's weird, but back in those days, so many people buried their heads in the sand and pretended that problems did not exist (even when they did). I had been one of those people, but no more.

---
1. See *Testimony of a Kept Woman*, pp.115-121

My mother-in-law was devastated about the divorce and that I was no longer married to her son, but that's how it had to be. She knew Vincent as well as I did. Now, for once in my life, I did what was best for me, and she understood.

Vincent's mother died in 2007 at the age of ninety-eight. She had called me before she died and asked that I attend her funeral with her two grandsons. I think she knew the possibilities of her son attending her funeral were minimal. She had continued to live in Philadelphia, and at the time we lived in other states. When she passed away, Dexter, Lawrence and I flew to their grandmother's and my former mother-in-love's funeral. Incredible as it was, Vincent was still angry and refused to attend his own mother's funeral! For me, that was the straw that broke the camel's back. I was totally disgusted with him and vowed never to speak to him again. Oh, but the Holy Spirit had different plans.

Defiant, Then Obedient

Soon after I returned home from the funeral, the Holy Spirit began to gently, but persistently speak to me in that quiet and still voice. He told me to call Vincent and witness to him over the phone. I was shocked and confused that the Lord would demand that I reach out to a man who had been so mean and insensitive to his own mother.

At first, I tried to ignore God's voice. I was totally resistant

Epilogue

to the idea that God would ask me to do something I was so opposed to doing. Secondly, God knew that I hadn't seen or heard from Vincent in over thirty-one years since I left him in Gary in 1976. What if Vincent wouldn't even answer the phone or talk to me?

After about five or six weeks, I eventually decided to be obedient and answer God's command. I called Vincent on a Sunday afternoon.[2]

THE AMAZING GRACE OF GOD

It was amazing! For more than two and a half hours, I talked to Vincent, Husband Number One, about the Gospel of Jesus Christ. I told my former physically violent and emotionally and verbally abusive husband of almost twenty years how much God the Father loved him. I told him that God loved him so much that He had sent His only begotten Son Jesus Christ to die for him and save him and I shared John 3:16 with him. I told him that God was offering him a gift of grace and share Ephesians 2:8-9 with him:

> *For it is by grace you have been saved, through faith—and this is not from yourselves, it is the gift of God—not by works so that no one can boast.*   Ephesians 2:8-9

---

2. See *Testimony of a Kept Woman*, pp.237-243

I told Vincent that all he had to do was to accept this precious gift.

To my amazement, Vincent listened intently to every word I was saying. He only interrupted occasionally to ask me questions, and, miraculously, I was able to answer his every question without stammering or hesitation. I told him the Good News of Jesus Christ without wavering. Of course, that was only by the help of the Holy Spirit. It was a phenomenal moment!

Slowly Vincent's hard heart began to melt, as he listened attentively to every word. After witnessing to Vincent for more than two hours over the phone, I asked him if he would like to pray the prayer of salvation and ask the Lord Jesus to save him. I fully expected Vincent to say no. After all, I had tried to witness to him while we were married years earlier, but unsuccessfully. This time was different. To my surprise, Vincent said yes to my offer! He said he wanted Jesus to save him!

I could hardly believe my ears! I nearly fainted with excitement and pleasure! I wanted to do a cartwheel and shout "Hallelujah!" I didn't because I didn't want to give Vincent a chance to change his mind. I quietly prayed the prayer of salvation with him, and he accepted the Lord Jesus Christ as His Savior over the phone.

Epilogue

Instantly, Vincent was born again, and he became a Christian (see Romans 10:9-10 and 13). To my great amazement, Vincent was not only converted; he was instantly transformed. Not only did he become a brand-new man in Christ Jesus, but Vincent changed all at once. He began to weep with loud sobs of joy! He then started laughing almost hysterically! Then Vincent shouted, "I feel as if a big boulder has been lifted off my shoulders and off my chest. I feel so free! I feel so light! I feel like I might just float up to the ceiling! I feel wonderful!" I was left speechless!

Then the most incredible thing happened! Vincent began to apologize to me over and over again. He told me that he was sorry for all the terrible things he had done to me and for having mistreated me all those years. It was as if scales had suddenly fallen from his eyes, and he could spiritually see clearly for the first time in his life. I was totally flabbergasted! It was truly a miracle!

Vincent's transformation was as dramatic and miraculous as the conversion of the apostle Paul on the rRoad to Damascus in Acts 9:1-19. I was shocked and overjoyed at the same time! It's unbelievable but true!

God does work in mysterious ways! His wonders to perform! And His timing is always perfect

From Victim to Victory

> *There is a time for everything,*
> *and a season for every activity under the heavens.*
>
> Ecclesiastes 3:1

All during those almost twenty years we had been married, I had prayed over and over for the Lord to change Vincent, but God did not answer my prayer. Nothing ever seemed to change the man, but I never stopped praying, even after we had long divorced and I moved on. Then, incredibly, the Lord finally answered my prayer, thirty-one years after I divorced Vincent. It was so unbelievable!

It is true that God does not always answer when we want Him to, but the Lord will always answer. You can count on that.

SWORD SHARPENING SWORD (PROVERBS 27:17).
The next day after I led Vincent to the Lord, I sent him a Bible, and we agreed to study the Bible together over the phone. It was wonderful! Only the Lord Jesus Christ could have changed Vincent from an angry and physically and verbally violent domestic abuser into a Bible-loving and gentle man who made peace with me and his two sons and bonded with his two granddaughters.

For the next ten years, Vincent and I continued our study of the Bible over the phone on the last Sunday of every month

Epilogue

promptly at 3:00 pm his time in Gary, Indiana (it was 4:00 pm my time in Greenville, North Carolina). Over a period of five years, I led Vincent to read and study the entire Bible, from Genesis to Revelation, chapter by chapter and verse by verse. His brilliant mind soaked up the scriptures like a sponge.

After we had completed the study of all sixty-six books of the Bible, Vincent took the lead, and for the next five years, he led the Bible lessons with skill and passion. He grew to love the Word of God. He memorized more than two hundred scriptures. We played challenging mental Bible drill games that he created to keep me on "my spiritual toes." His favorite scripture for our studies together was: *"As iron sharpens iron, so a friend sharpens a friend"* (Proverbs 27:17, NLT).

Vincent joined a health and fitness center in Gary and became one of its finest members. With his spiritual transformation, his personality also changed, and he gained friends. He led a small group at the center. In the mornings, they read scripture and recited a memorized Bible verse before they began their exercise regimen. Vincent enjoyed many happy hours at that center.

A Great Ending to a Transformed Life

On Thursday, January 19, 2017, I received a telephone call from Vincent's neighbor who lived across the street from him.

After he got saved, he had given her my number in case of an emergency. She informed me that Vincent had died suddenly from an apparent heart attack or stroke. With sadness, Dexter, Lawrence and I flew to Gary and took care of his final arrangements.

With Vincent's complete conversion and transformation, his behavior had radically changed. He had not only made peace with his sons; he had developed a warm and loving relationship with his two granddaughters (Lawrence's children). We all mourned Vincent's death, but the Lord gave us a tranquil closure to end a relationship that had begun so poorly. We were at peace, knowing that Vincent had gone on to Glory to be with the God he loved.

A Final Thought-Provoking Note:

It's interesting to realize that all the contacts I had with Vincent during those many years were made via telephone. I never personally saw him again after we had separated and divorced in 1976. Still, his life and mine became reconnected when the Spirit spoke to me after his mother's funeral to call him and witness to him over the phone. I didn't want to do it, and I was rebellious for a period of time. Thank God, after six weeks of prodding, I was finally obedient, and my obedience had yielded eternal fruit.

Epilogue

Yes, it is true that *"obedience is better than sacrifice"* (1 Samuel 15:22, MEV) and *"rebellion is as the sin of witchcraft!"* (1 Samuel 15:23, KJV). Thank God for His Word, for the "Phone Ministry," and the invention of the technology that made it all possible. Our Lord Jesus Christ is awesome!

TO GOD BE THE GLORY!

And we know that in all things God works for the good of those who love him, who have been called according to his purpose.   Romans 8:28

Special Features

WHAT IS REAL LOVE?

What is love?

Is love a feeling, a choice, a decision, an action, a noun, or a verb?

What is love?

Is love an expression of various emotions: happiness, sadness, surprises, pain, or heartache?

What is love?

My definition of love had been based on Hollywood and what I observed in other people. Unfortunately, I did not have a true definition of what should last a lifetime, because I was looking for love in all the wrong places. I found the definition of love in a place that I only ran to out of fear, desperation, and anxiety.

What is real love?

The definition of REAL LOVE can only be found in the Word of God derived from the search of the One Who is the epitome of LOVE, God Himself. Here's what His Word, His love letter to us, says about love:

> 1 Corinthians 13:4-8, KJV
> *Charity suffereth long, and is kind; charity envieth not; charity vaunteth not itself, is not puffed up, doth not behave itself unseemly, seeketh not her own, is not easily provoked, thinketh no evil; rejoiceth not in iniquity, but rejoiceth in the truth; beareth all things, believeth all things, hopeth all things, endureth all things. Charity never faileth.*

> 1 Corinthians 13:4-8, ESV
> *Love is patient and kind; love does not envy or boast; it is not arrogant or rude. It does not insist on its own way; it is not irritable or resentful; it does not rejoice at wrongdoing, but rejoices with the truth. Love bears all things, believes all things, hopes all things, endures all things.*
> *Love never ends.*

> 1 Corinthians 13:4-8
> *Love is patient, love is kind. It does not envy, it does not boast, it is not proud. It does not dishonor others, it is not self-seeking, it is not easily angered, it keeps no record of wrongs. Love does not delight in evil but rejoices with*

What Is Real Love?

the truth. It always protects, always trusts, always hopes, always perseveres.
Love never fails.

1 Corinthians 13:4-8, MSG
> Love never gives up.
> Love cares more for others than for self.
> Love doesn't want what it doesn't have.
> Love doesn't strut,
> Doesn't have a swelled head,
> Doesn't force itself on others,
> Isn't always "me first,"
> Doesn't fly off the handle,
> Doesn't keep score of the sins of others,
> Doesn't revel when others grovel,
> Takes pleasure in the flowering of truth,
> Puts up with anything,
> Trusts God always,
> Always looks for the best,
> Never looks back,
> But keeps going to the end.
> Love never dies.

1 Corinthians 13:4-8, AMP
> Love endures with patience and serenity, love is kind and thoughtful, and is not jealous or envious; love does not

> *brag and is not proud or arrogant. It is not rude; it is not self-seeking, it is not provoked [nor overly sensitive and easily angered]; it does not take into account a wrong endured. It does not rejoice at injustice, but rejoices with the truth [when right and truth prevail]. Love bears all things [regardless of what comes], believes all things [looking for the best in each one], hopes all things [remaining steadfast during difficult times], endures all things [without weakening].*
> *Love never fails [it never fades nor ends].*

We are never more like our Creator and Lover than when we love another human being as we love ourselves.

What is love?
  GOD is REAL LOVE!

> *He that loveth not knoweth not God; for God is love.*
> 1 John 4:8, KJV

WHY DOES SHE STAY?

The LORD is near to the brokenhearted
and saves those who are crushed in spirit.
Psalm 34:18, NASB

The Universal Question Is: Why Does She Stay? Why Doesn't She Just Leave?

One of the most frequently asked questions of victims of domestic abuse by people who have never experienced it themselves is, "Why does she stay? Why doesn't she just leave?" You may have even asked this question yourself. Sometimes we ask this question because we actually don't understand what might be keeping someone in a terrible relationship. At other times, this issue might be used as a way to blame the woman for the abuse she receives.

This universal problem is both paradoxical and complicated. People who have never been abused by a spouse or intimate partner often say that if their partner ever abused them, they certainly would leave. They say, "It would only take one time, and I'd be outta here!"

That sounds brave and heroic, but truthfully speaking, it's easier said than done. I know because I was a victim of both physical violence and emotional and verbal abuse for a total of forty-two years—almost two decades with Husband number one (physical violence) and twenty-two years with Husband Number Two (emotional and verbal abuse).

Victims of domestic violence are not always passive. They are employing survival techniques every day to protect themselves and their children–everything short of leaving. Staying in or returning to an abusive relationship is a difficult choice to make because the decision to leave might have life-threatening consequences. According to statistics, the majority of victims of domestic violence are murdered by their abusers during or after their attempt to escape.

As you read through the various reasons why victims of domestic abuse choose to stay or return to dysfunctional and dangerous relationships, hopefully you will be able to better appreciate the plight of someone living in these desperate circumstances. Once you are equipped with more awareness and insight regarding a victim's crazy world, then perhaps you will discover that what you once thought were unreasonable

Why Does She Stay?

and irrational reasons to stay in domestic violence might just begin to make a little more sense to you. Let's begin.

Countless victims of domestic abuse stay and do not leave their abusers because of the following reasons:

1. **The cycle of ill-treatment gives the victim hope for positive change.**
Victims are often anchored by the hope that the person they fell in love with—the sweet, gentle and caring one—will prevail over the abusive person who is causing them harm.

2. **The victim may be dependent on her abusive partner.**
For many victims, their economic or social well-being may be on the line when walking away from their abuser.

3. **Leaving could mean more violence.**
Many abusive partners will levy threats of further and more extreme violence against the victim as a way to stop them from reporting abuse or leaving a relationship. For victims, walking away isn't always easy; it can be a decision that puts them in extreme danger.

4. **Victims want to protect their children.**
Victims who have children have to take those children into account when they prepare to leave. Some abusive partners will harm or threaten to harm their partner's children if a

survivor reports their abuse to the authorities or confesses their experiences to someone they trust. This is true even if those children are also the abuser's.

5. **Victims often lack support.**

Victims of abuse may not be supported by their friends and family, their local police, or a judge or jury when they attempt to seek justice and escape their abuser.

6. **Victims may have limited financial resources.**

If the victim shares a joint bank account with her abuser, it's hard for her to break free. Some abusers may even take a victim's paycheck from them or create a very strict budget to try to ensure that the victim is unable to leave without ending up on the streets. When combined with the lack of a strong support network, this can make it almost impossible to make the break.

7. **Victims may have limited work experience.**

If the victim has been a stay-at-home mom or hasn't been allowed to keep a steady job by her partner, this can make the idea of breaking free even more intimidating. It can be difficult to find a job that pays enough to allow her to escape—especially if children are part of the equation.

8. **Victims have unanswered questions about child custody and child support.**

It's easy to be frustrated or even angry with women who don't remove their children from an abusive environment. Unfortunately, sometimes the only alternative is that the victim might be unable to support her children at all—or that sole custody will actually be given to the abusive parent or to the State.

9. **Victims may not be able to take a pet with them.**
Many men actually keep their partners in line by threatening the victim's pets. If a woman's only option is to go to a shelter where her pet isn't allowed, her fears for the animal's safety may keep her from leaving. She may not have any options for temporary pet care while she works on becoming more independent.

10. **Victims may be afraid of being alone.**
Obviously, it's better to be alone than to be in a relationship that hurts you, but many victims of physical and emotional abuse have been convinced over the course of their relationship that no one else could possibly want them. When you actually believe that you may never find someone else, it's possible to rationalize away some seriously twisted behavior.

11. **In some cases, the victim's family or community agency pressures keep her from leaving.**
If the victim belongs to a religion that frowns upon divorce or if family members have strong relationships with the abuser, they may pressure the victim to try to work things

out. This social pressure can make the victim feel guilty for wanting to leave and keep her from accessing the resources she would need to make a clean break.

12. **Victims feel guilty for "causing" the abuse.**
A common tactic abusers like to use is listing all the reasons why the victim's behavior provoked them. Believe it or not, hearing this over and over again can actually make the victim start to doubt her own sanity—making her question her version of events. Victims will often find themselves walking on eggshells and trying desperately to avoid behaviors they believe will cause more abuse.

13. **Sometimes the victim's relationship may seem healthy.**
Some abusers will go weeks or months between violent or manipulative episodes. They may appear genuinely remorseful about their bad behavior and claim they're willing to change. A woman in this type of relationship may believe that the abuse really won't happen again—or that it's worth sticking through the bad parts because the rest of the relationship makes her happy.

14. **The victim may be afraid of provoking additional violence.**
It's a sad statistic, but 75% of women who are killed by their partners are murdered during or after an attempt to leave the

relationship. If the choice is between a black eye or death, sometimes the smart choice is to stay put.

15. **The victim loves her abusive partner, and love is a powerful force.**
Spousal abuse and intimate partner violence are unique because it occurs in a relationship, and relationships themselves are emotionally involved.

16. **The victim lacks self-esteem or confidence.**
Ending an intimate relationship is almost always difficult, but even more so when the victim's self-confidence has been destroyed by an abuser.

17. **The victim believes the myths about domestic violence.**
Victims of domestic violence may assume that violence in an unavoidable part of their life. Victims may also blame themselves for the violence as they are repeatedly told it is their fault by their abuser. The victim becomes convinced and believes that it's her responsibility to "fix" the craziness.

18. **The victim is committed to the relationship.**
The abuser is the person the victim loves. This makes leaving the abuser particularly challenging where violent episodes are followed by periods of affection and positive attention. The abuser may be the father of the victim's children. The

victim may want to end the violence but also seeks to preserve the family relationship. The victim may also be bound by religious implications of marriage, and there may be other reasons related to maintaining the relationship to consider.

19. **The victim has no place to go/fear of homelessness.**
Sad, but true, there are more animal shelters in the U.S. than shelters for battered women and children. Domestic violence is the cause of half of the homelessness in America's women and children.

20. **The victim is isolated.**
Many victims of domestic violence do not have a support system. The abuser has systematically isolated the victim. For example, the abuser may prohibit the victim from using the phone, may humiliate her at family gatherings, may insist on transporting her to and from work, or may censor her mail, email, texting, and cellphone records. Abusers are often highly possessive.

21. **The victim is in denial.**
Victims of domestic violence fear that no one will believe that their partners abuse them. Abusers are often charismatic figures, ingratiating and attractive in the community, while keeping their terrorizing and controlling behaviors within the family and behind closed doors.

22. **The victim's life is in danger when attempting to leave.**
Many victims believe that leaving is not going to make their life and their children's lives any safer. As noted, many victims of domestic violence are killed by their partners after they have left the abuser. Leaving can be a dangerous process. Many abusers escalate their violence to coerce the victim into reconciliation or to retaliate for the victim's departure.

23. **The victim is in economic dependence.**
The most likely indicator of whether a victim of domestic violence will permanently separate from her abuser is whether she has the financial resources to survive without the abuser.

24. **The victim is ashamed or embarrassed.**
Although abuse is never the victim's fault, many victims feel ashamed that someone is hurting them. Victims may believe, "This doesn't happen to people like me."

25. **Leaving is a process.**
Most victims of domestic violence leave and return several times before permanently separating from the abuser. The first time a victim leaves may be a test to see whether the abuser will obtain help or stop his abuse.

The problems of domestic abuse are similar, but no two situations are exactly the same. Motives and escape plans will vary significantly. Therefore, the twenty-five reasons listed here are not exhaustive but are an attempt to give clarification and an explanation for why victims stay and do not leave their abusers.

The next time you are tempted to ask that universal question. "Why does she stay?" remember that victimization isn't simplistic or logical.

A PRAYER FOR THOSE NOT IN ABUSIVE RELATIONSHIPS
"Lord, I thank You. There, but for the grace of God, go I."

Web Resources:
http://www.stopviolence.com/domviol/WhySheSometimesStays.pdf
http://www.huffingtonpost.com/2014/09/12/why-didnt-you-just-leave_n_5805134.html
http://www.peacefromdv.org/why-does-she-stay/
https://www.azmag.gov/archive/DV/About_DV/Profile/profile.html
http://ndvsac.org/dv/why-does-she-stay/
https://www.ted.com/talks/leslie_morgan_steiner_why_domestic_violence_victims_don_t_leave
http://newchoicesinc.org/educated/abuse/dv/whynotleave
http://ncadv.org/learn-more/statistics
http://www.cdvs.com.au/about-3/about-domestic-violence/the-effects-of-domestic-violence-on-families/why-women-stay/
http://www.faithtrustinstitute.org/resources/learn-the-basics/dv-faqs

BATTERED MEN
(THE SILENT VICTIMS IN DOMESTIC VIOLENCE)

*The LORD tests the righteous,
but his soul hates the wicked and the one who loves
violence.*   Psalm 11:5, ESV

*Repay no one evil for evil, but give thought to do what
is honorable in the sight of all. If possible, so far as it
depends on you, live peaceably with all.*
                                      Romans 12:17-18, ESV

DOMESTIC VIOLENCE AND ABUSED MEN

Domestic abuse–both physical violence and emotional and verbal abuse—is a pervasive and growing problem in our society. The vast majority of victims are women. However, men are being abused by women more often than most people suspect. Typically, men are physically stronger than women, and that makes it easier for them to escape the violence or the relationship. However, that is not necessarily true in all cases.

Why are Men Becoming Victims of Domestic Violence?

In today's society, the roles of men and women are becoming increasingly blurred and troubling, as women are moving more into the man's world. Women also earn and compete as aggressively and vigorously as their male colleagues. It is my opinion that more married men suffer abuse from their spouses than married women. It's also problematic that women are fast catching up with men in the consumption of alcohol. Thus, female-on-male domestic violence is on the rise.

The official statistics of men who are victims of domestic violence is significantly underestimated because men are reluctant to say that they've been abused by a woman. It makes them appear to be unmanly and weak. Male victims are often treated as "second-class victims" in society. Many police forces and councils do not take them seriously. Male victims of domestic abuse are almost invisible to the various governmental agencies. Rarely can authorities be counted on to take an objective look at the man's side of the problem. The plight of men who suffer in domestic abuse is also widely overlooked by the media, in official reports, and in governmental policies.

Although more and more men are being becoming victims of domestic violence, they are not being treated equally. Society and agencies continue to adopt the gendered analysis that so many in the domestic violence establishment still pursue, that the primary focus should be female victims. However, each victim, whether male or female, should be seen as an individual and helped accordingly.

What Types of Abuse are Committed by Females Against Male Victims?

Studies of spousal and dating violence indicate that women are as likely as men to assault their partners physically. Younger women in their twenties are significantly more likely to aggressively attack men than women who are thirty years old and above.

Women abuse their male partners by:

- Pushing them
- Slapping them
- Hitting them
- Biting them
- Throwing objects at them
- Threatening them with weapons
- Etc.

However, the domestic abuse inflicted by females is not only or necessarily physical. To make up for any difference in physical strength, women sometimes strategically attack the male while he is asleep or otherwise catch the victim by surprise.

From Victim to Victory

Other ways women hurt men include:
- Verbally abusing him
- Belittling or humiliating him in front of friends, colleagues, or family, or on social media sites
- Acting possessive or jealous
- Harassing him with accusations of unfaithfulness
- Hiding or taking away his car keys or medications
- Attempting to destroy his reputation
- Controlling where he goes and who he sees
- Attempting to spend money or deliberately default on mutual financial obligations
- Making false allegations about him to his friends, his employer, or the police
- Finding ways to manipulate and isolate him
- Threatening to leave and preventing him from seeing his children if the abuse is reported
- Emotionally humiliating him, especially in public
- Inflicting severe emotional damage on him
- Disrespecting him
- Making accusations that he is a failure or a coward
- Resorting to name calling
- Using hurtful and accusatory words to inflict psychological and emotional damage on him
- Abusing or threatening his children
- Harming his pets

Battered Men

WHY IS IT DIFFICULT TO RECOGNIZE MEN WHO ARE BATTERED BY WOMEN?

There are statistics to support an estimated number of men being abused, but these cannot be accurate because most men never report the incidences. It's difficult to identify a male who is a victim of domestic abuse. For one thing, social service agencies and advocates have done little to encourage men to report incidents of domestic abuse.

Another difficulty is that there are numerous resources for women who are victims of abuse, but few for men. The community as a whole has done little or nothing to address the problem of male victimization.

The actual harm done to men, in most cases of domestic abuse, is more emotional than physical. Also, the impact on the community isn't as high. However, the attached stigma prevents many men from reporting abuse by their spouses. If someone has suffered a noticeable injury, most people assume it was caused by another man or by playing sports. Many people would not believe a woman could inflict an injury so severe.

WHAT CATEGORIES OF WOMEN ARE MOST PRONE TO DOMESTIC VIOLENCE AGAINST MEN?

Women who are abusers generally fall into one of three categories:

- **Alcoholics:** Many women who abuse their spouses are alcoholics, and the alcohol is responsible for triggering their violence.

- **Psychologically Troubled:** Women with personality disorders are often violent and abusive. Their disorder also causes them to lie, become suicidal, have mood swings, or be prone to alcohol or drug abuse.

- **Women with Unrealistic Expectations:** Some women with unrealistic expectations blame their emotional state (which may actually have been caused by past trauma or drugs or alcohol) on their husband or partner. They feel there's something wrong with their partner, not them. When their man doesn't meet their expectations, they turn on him.

A True Story of Male Victimization

Michelle Mills was impeccably groomed and had a pleasant demeanor and yet she subjected her husband, Edward, to an onslaught of violence. He was often scratched, punched, and screamed at. One day, Michelle, brandishing a kitchen knife, stabbed him to death in the living room of their picturesque cottage in the lovely village of Scalford, Leicestershire, England. Her attack was so ferocious that the knife blade broke away from the handle. On April 26, 2013, Michelle was convicted of murder and was sentenced to life in prison.

Why Do Men Remain in Abusive Relationships? What Doesn't He Just Leave?

If many have trouble understanding why a woman who is being abused by her husband or boyfriend doesn't just get up and leave, it is even more confusing if the victim is a male. However, anyone who's been in an abusive relationship knows that it's never a simple thing to pack up and go. Ending a relationship, even an abusive one, is rarely easy. Some possible reasons men might remain in an abusive relationship are:

- He somehow feels it's his fault.
- He blames himself for events in the past that he had no control over but is assuming responsibility for.
- He may feel dependent on his wife, either emotionally or financially.
- He is afraid his wife will tell the children he's a bad person.
- He is afraid of losing sole custody of the children and not being able to see them again.
- He knows that few of the resources available to battered women are available for men.
- He wants to protect his children.
- He feels ashamed.
- His religious beliefs won't let him walk away from his marriage.
- He lacks financial resources.
- He is in denial.

A Spotlight on a Female Abuser: "For 13 years, He Never Hit Her Back."

> For 13 years, Karen Gillhespy was the abuser. She says she broke her husband's ribs, ripped entire patches of his hair out, scratched him, bit him, beat him with a baseball bat, and kicked him. He never hit back, and he never filed charges against her.
>
> But even more shocking to Gillhepsy are the reactions she encountered telling her story. "They told me I was the victim," said Gillhespy, thirty-four, of Marquette [Michigan]. "There's no way any of this was his fault. I knew the difference between being the victim and being the perpetrator. I am ashamed of what I did."
>
> Gillhespy believes most people don't believe men can be victims. She knows they are wrong. "I think it is just as dangerous as [violence against women]. You just don't hear about it," Gillhespy says. "Maybe more men would come forward if you did."
>
> Gillhespy, who wed at 16, says she began beating her husband early in their 16-year marriage. Her

former husband, reached by phone, declined to comment but confirmed that abuse took place. At the time, Gillhespy was a crack user, heroin addict, and alcoholic. She says she beat her husband in fits of rage, usually when she wanted money or the car. "I told him he was no good and that he was a loser. I kicked him and threw things at him," the wife said. "I used him and used him and used him."

The turning point came in February 1993, when Gillhespy struck two pregnant women in Grand Rapids while driving drunk. Gillhespy received 45 days in jail and was sent to a drug treatment program in Marquette. She has gotten a divorce, finished high school, and stayed sober. In a year, she will receive a degree from Northern Michigan University. And although Gillhespy now understands the issues that led her to violence, she says she accepts full responsibility for her actions. Her strength, she says, comes from admitting that she had a problem — and from trying to help others recognize that domestic violence goes both ways.

"I'm the other side of the coin," she says. *"If you're abused, you're abused."*[1]

WHY DO MEN HESITATE TO SPEAK UP ABOUT BEING ABUSED?

In a male-dominated society, it's hard for a victimized man to talk about his experience with violence to the authorities. Therefore, men are suffering from domestic abuse, and it happens to men from all cultures and all walks of life. Figures suggest that as many as one in three victims of domestic violence are male. However, men are often reluctant to report abuse by women because they feel embarrassed, or they fear they won't be believed, or worse, that police will assume that since they are male, they are the perpetrator of the violence and not the victim.[2]

When a man is the person being abused, he's not as likely to speak up because of the stigma attached. He may feel that no one will believe him or that he's exaggerating the situation. Very often, men have no one to turn to, or if they did, they'd find it difficult to express that they're being controlled by a woman. Male victims are almost invisible to the authorities. Abuse of men has risen sharply in the last few years, but no one knows exactly how many cases there are, since many men don't commonly report incidents.

---

1. A *Detroit News* report by Becky Beaupre. http://www.batteredmen.com/detbatm2.htm
2. Special Report: No place to run for male victims of domestic abuse: Shelters, support groups rare for men whose mates batter them at home. A *Detroit News* report by Becky Beaupre.

Battered Men

How Can Men Protect Themselves Against Abusive Females in Relationships?

Men must use wisdom in dealing with an abusive partner by doing the following:

- **Leave if possible.** Be aware of any signs that may trigger a violent response from your spouse or partner and be ready to move quickly. If you need to stay to protect your children, call emergency services. The police have an obligation to protect you and your children, just as they do a female victim.

- **Never retaliate physically.** An abusive woman or partner will often try to provoke you into retaliating or using force to escape the situation. If you do retaliate, you'll almost certainly be the one who is arrested and/or removed from your home.

- **Get evidence of the abuse.** Report all incidents to the police and get a copy of each police report. Keep a journal of all abuse with a clear record of dates, times, and any witnesses. Include a photographic record of your injuries and make sure your doctor or hospital also documents your injuries. Remember, medical personnel are unlikely to ask if a man has been a victim of domestic violence, so it's up to you to ensure that the cause of your injuries is documented.

- **Keep a mobile phone, evidence of the abuse, and other important documents close at hand.** If you and your children have to leave quickly to escape abuse, you'll need to take with you evidence of the abuse and relevant documents, such as passport, and driver's license. It may be safer to keep these items outside of the home.

- **Obtain professional advice.** This could be from an attorney and/or domestic violence program or legal-aid resource. They may advise you to get a restraining order or order of protection against your spouse and, if necessary, seek temporary custody of your children.

What Tips are Available for Abused Men?

Abused men can reach out to the following organizations, by calling for help:

- The National Domestic Abuse Hotline (800-799-SAFE) or the National Child Abuse Hotline (800 4-A-CHILD).

- Call 911 or your local emergency service.
- In the U.S. and Canada, call The National Domestic Violence Hotline (800-799-7233).

- In the UK, call ManKind Initiative (01823 334244) or Men's Advice Line(0808 801 0327).

Battered Men

- In Australia, visit One in Three Campaign for advice and hotlines.

- Worldwide, visit Safe Horizon for a list of crisis hotlines, shelters, and other resources or International Directory of Domestic Violence Agencies.

How Should Men Move on from an Abusive Relationship?

After the trauma of an abusive relationship, it can take a while to get over the pain and bad memories, but you can heal and move on.

When considering moving on and entering a new relationship and finally get the intimacy and support you crave, it is wise to take things slowly. Make sure you're aware of any red flag behaviors in a potential new partner and what is needed to build healthy, new relationships.

Web Resources
http://www.mintpressnews.com/woman-aggressor-unspoken-truth-domestic-violence/196746/
http://www.bbc.com/news/uk-england-leicestershire-22350941
http://www.mintpressnews.com/woman-aggressor-unspoken-truth-domestic-violence/196746/
https://www.helpguide.org/articles/abuse/help-for-abused-men.htm
http://www.mneweb.org/fiebert.htm) http://www.batteredmen.com/sethatm2.htm
http://www.crimeandinvestigation.com.uk/crime-files/the-murder-of-edward-miller

SEVEN PRICELESS PRINCIPLES
(HOW TO RAISE FUNCTIONAL KIDS IN A DYSFUNCTIONAL ENVIRONMENT)

Train up a child in the way he should go, and when he is old, he will not depart from it.
Proverbs 22:6, KJV

The study of the book of Proverbs not only makes you healthy, wealthy, and wise; it will give you excellent parenting skills that have been proven by time. King Solomon is the author of the book, and he wrote it in a unique and simple way—like a calendar. There are 31 days in a month, and there are 31 chapters in the book of Proverbs. Therefore, you can begin reading a chapter anytime by simply reading whatever day of the week it happens to be.

For example, if today is the 3rd of the month, then read Proverbs 3. If the day of week is the 28th, then read Proverbs 28.

Seven Priceless Principles

It is not necessary to read the entire chapter that day. Solomon's proverbs are packed with wise advice about working hard, guarding your tongue, avoiding bad friendships, and handling money well. Read for quality rather than quantity. It's not about how much you read as much as how much you retain and apply.

In the study of Proverbs, you will not only gain parenting skills, but you will also discover that "a verse a day can keep the devil away."

How to Raise Functional Kids in a Dysfunctional Environment

My parents used these principles on my sister and me, and I used these same principles to raise my three good (not ~~perfect~~) children. The beauty and practicality of these seven P's is that they are all free, and yet they are priceless. They will pay high dividends in your child's life and future. I guarantee it!

These seven amazing keys will not cost you one dime. Raising functional kids is not about spending money. The secret is spending time now.

What Are the Seven Keys for Raising Functional Kids in a Dysfunctional Environment?

1. Prayer

Pray *with* your children and pray *for* your children. Get down on your knees with them at night and pray before they go to bed. As parents, let your children see you praying and reading your Bible at home. This is a powerful mental image they will never forget.

2. Patience

Show parental patience and love through discipline. The Bible says, *"Whoever spares the rod hates their children, but the one who loves their children is careful to discipline them.* (Proverbs 13:24). Do not delegate this responsibility to the school and others. Be gentle and not harsh, but teach your children how to respect you and the Lord. It takes time and patience to raise godly children, but wise parents will discipline their children promptly and consistently.

3. Protection

Protect the physical body and the minds of your children from the filth of this world. Carefully monitor what goes into the eye-gate and ear-gate of your kids. Watch and listen to what they see and hear on TV, technology gadgets, and computer games. Do not allow your children to view or participate in activities until they have reached the maturity level needed to absorb and understand the concept.

4. Preparation

Prepare and arrange your family life with consistent, regular, and orderly scheduled days. Have specific times to eat, sleep, work, and play. Go to bed on time, wake up on time, and go to school and to work on time. Model punctuality and good work habits in front of your children, and they will emulate what they see their parents do.

5. Persistence

Persistently teach the principles you want your children to learn by demonstrating them yourself. Do not say one thing and do something else in front of your kids. Teach them to tell the truth by not lying to them. Teach them self-control by being in control of your own emotions and passions.

6. Participation

Spend time with your children. Participate with them in their school activities. Take them to church and Sunday School. Talk often and freely with them. Listen to them carefully. Let them know you are interested in what they think and what they do. Remember, the best thing you can spend on your children is TIME. Care enough to be there for them, as much as is possible.

7. Praise

Accentuate the positive and reduce the negative comments. Praise more and criticize less. Intentionally look for your children's strengths and encourage them rather than condemning them for their faults and weaknesses. That is what our heavenly Father does for each of us.

Please note, PROVISION was intentionally omitted from this list. Every good parent is expected to provide materially, but also emotionally, physically, and psychologically. Provision is understood.

Some parents are able to provide better than others based on economics (money), but money does not determine your success or lack of success in parenting. That is why this list is doable for everyone.

Interestingly enough, no money is needed to achieve these seven principles. Every parent, regardless of educational background or social-economic status, can activate the list.

Again, the best thing parents can SPEND on their children is TIME. Why? Because you don't get any do-overs in raising children. Do it right NOW and you can enjoy the benefits LATER. Your children will become your SECURITY BLANKET instead of your GUILT TRIP. God Himself said:

> *Train up a child in the way he should go, and when he is old, he will not depart from it.*
>
> Proverbs 22:6, KJV

SIX STEPS ON THE ROMAN ROAD TO SALVATION

From Victim to Victory: How To Recover from the Trauma and Drama of Domestic Abuse is based on the principles of being a child of the true and living God. Only a Christian can experience complete recovery and deliverance from pain and brokenness without anger and bitterness. Why? Because only a Christian has access to the power of the Spirit of God, who alone **"heals the brokenhearted and binds up their wounds"** (Psalm 147:3).

When you are broken and in despair, you feel as though you are all alone. It is in times like these that you might ask the question, "Does God really care about me?" The answer is Yes, God absolutely loves and cares for you. The Bible says, **"He who did not spare his own Son but gave him up for us all, how will He not also with him graciously give us all things?"** (Romans 8:32). It is a great comfort to know that God *"will never leave you nor forsake you"* (Hebrews 13:5, NKJV).

God is always near to comfort the believer. ***"Blessed be the God and Father of our Lord Jesus Christ, the Father of mercies and God of all comfort, who comforts us in all our affliction"*** (2 Corinthians 1:3-4, ESV).

God cannot lie. Whatever the Lord says must come to fruition. Whatever He has promised, He will do, and Jesus has promised to go through our trials with us. ***"When you pass through the waters, I will be with you; and through the rivers, they shall not overwhelm you; when you walk through fire you shall not be burned, and the flame shall not consume you"*** (Isaiah 43:2, ESV).

God has never failed one of His people when they cried out to Him, and He will not fail the heartbroken Christian who cries out to Him today. He may not always answer exactly in the way we would like, but He answers according to His perfect will and timing. And, while we are waiting for the answer, His grace is sufficient for us (see 2 Corinthians 12:9).

If you are not a child of the Most High God, our heavenly Father, you can become His child. He has made it possible for you to come to the Father through His only begotten Son, Jesus Christ. It requires what has come to be called "Six Steps on the Romans Road to Salvation."

Six Steps on the Roman Road to Salvation

WHAT ARE THE SIX STEPS ON THE ROMAN ROAD TO SALVATION?

The six steps on the Romans road to salvation are an easy and effective way of explaining the Good News of salvation. This method uses verses from the book of Romans, and is a simple, yet powerful, method of explaining why we need salvation, how God provided salvation, how we can receive salvation, and what the results of salvation are.

HERE ARE THE SIX STEPS:

Step #1. The first verse on the Romans Road to Salvation is Romans 3:23, ***"For all have sinned, and come short of the glory of God"*** (KJV). We have all sinned. We have all done things that are displeasing to God. No one is innocent. Romans 3:10-18 gives a detailed picture of what sin looks like in our lives.

Step #2. The second scripture on the Romans Road to Salvation is Romans 6:23. It teaches us about the consequences of sin: ***"For the wages of sin is death"*** (KJV). The punishment we have earned for our sins is death, not just physical death, but eternal death!

Step #3. The third verse on the Romans Road to Salvation is Romans 6:23, ***"but the gift of God is eternal life through***

Jesus Christ our Lord" (KJV). Romans 5:8 declares, *"But God demonstrates His own love toward us, in that while we were still sinners, Christ died for us"* (MEV). Jesus Christ died for us, and His death paid the price for our sins. Jesus' resurrection proves that God accepted the death of His Son, Jesus, as the payment for our sins.

Step #4. The fourth verse on the Romans Road to Salvation is Romans 10:9-10, *"that if you confess with your mouth Jesus as Lord, and believe in your heart that God raised Him from the dead, you will be saved. For with the heart one believes unto righteousness, and with the mouth confession is made unto salvation"* (NKJV). Because of Jesus' death on our behalf, all we have to do is believe in Him, trusting His death as the payment for our sins, and we will be saved! Romans 10:13 says it again, *"For whoever calls on the name of the Lord will be saved"* (NKJV). Jesus died to pay the penalty for our sins and rescue us from eternal death. Salvation, the forgiveness of sins, is available to anyone who will trust in Jesus Christ as their Lord and Savior.

Step #5. The fifth verse of the Romans Road to Salvation is the result of salvation. Romans 5:1 says, *"Therefore since we have been justified by faith, we have peace with God through our Lord Jesus Christ."* Through Jesus Christ, we can have a relationship of peace with God. Romans 8:1 teaches us, *"Therefore, there is now no condemnation for those who are in Christ Jesus."* Because of Jesus' death on our behalf, we will never be condemned for our sins.

Step #6. Finally, we have this precious promise of God from Romans 8:38-39, *"For I am convinced that neither death nor life, neither angels nor demons, neither the present nor the future, nor any powers, neither height nor depth, nor anything else in all creation, will be able to separate us from the love of God that is in Christ Jesus our Lord."*

Now that you know about the road to salvation through Jesus Christ, would you like to follow this Roman Road to Salvation? If your answer is yes, here is a simple prayer you can pray to God. Saying this prayer is a way to declare to Him that you are relying on Jesus Christ for your salvation. The words themselves will not save you. Only faith in Jesus Christ can provide salvation!

If you are ready, say this prayer of salvation out loud (see Romans 10:17):

Heavenly Father,

I know that I have sinned against You, and I deserve Your punishment. But Jesus Christ took the punishment that I deserve so that through faith in Him I could be forgiven. Father, I repent of my sins, and I place my trust in Your Son, Jesus Christ. I believe that He is the Son of God. Thank You for Your wonderful grace and forgiveness and the gift of eternal life! Thank You for saving me, Father.

Amen!

Praise God! If you have prayed the prayer of salvation, you are now saved and on your way to Heaven. Find and join a Bible-believing, Bible-teaching, and Bible-professing church, and grow in Jesus Christ.

Web Resources
http://www.gotquestions.org
http://www.stephenhowellenterprises.com
https://www.backtothebible.org/is-my-child-in-heaven
https://www.youtube.com/watch?v=KvF1QtgnurY

AUTHOR CONTACT PAGE

You may contact the author directly in the following way:

eMail: jannewellbyrd@gmail.com

www.ingramcontent.com/pod-product-compliance
Lightning Source LLC
Chambersburg PA
CBHW032042150426
43194CB00006B/384